Harvard
Business
Review

ON

TEAMS THAT SUCCEED

From the library of

Ellen Hart

THE HARVARD BUSINESS REVIEW PAPERBACK SERIES

The series is designed to bring today's managers and professionals the fundamental information they need to stay competitive in a fast-moving world. From the preeminent thinkers whose work has defined an entire field to the rising stars who will redefine the way we think about business, here are the leading minds and landmark ideas that have established the *Harvard Business Review* as required reading for ambitious businesspeople in organizations around the globe.

Other books in the series:

Harvard Business Review Interviews with CEOs

Harvard Business Review on Advances in Strategy

Harvard Business Review on Becoming a High Performance Manager

Harvard Business Review on Brand Management

Harvard Business Review on Breakthrough Leadership

Harvard Business Review on Breakthrough Thinking

Harvard Business Review on Building Personal and Organizational Resilience

Harvard Business Review on Business and the Environment

Harvard Business Review on the Business Value of IT

Harvard Business Review on Change

Harvard Business Review on Compensation

Harvard Business Review on Corporate Ethics

Harvard Business Review on Corporate Governance

Harvard Business Review on Corporate Responsibility

Harvard Business Review on Corporate Strategy

Harvard Business Review on Crisis Management

Harvard Business Review on Culture and Change

Harvard Business Review on Customer Relationship Management

Harvard Business Review on Decision Making

Other books in the series (continued):

Harvard Business Review on Developing Leaders
Harvard Business Review on Effective Communication
Harvard Business Review on Entrepreneurship
Harvard Business Review on Finding and Keeping the Best People
Harvard Business Review on Innovation
Harvard Business Review on the Innovative Enterprise
Harvard Business Review on Knowledge Management
Harvard Business Review on Leadership
Harvard Business Review on Leadership at the Top
Harvard Business Review on Leadership in a Changed World
Harvard Business Review on Leading in Turbulent Times
Harvard Business Review on Managing Diversity
Harvard Business Review on Managing High-Tech Industries
Harvard Business Review on Managing People
Harvard Business Review on Managing Uncertainty
Harvard Business Review on Managing the Value Chain
Harvard Business Review on Managing Your Career
Harvard Business Review on Marketing
Harvard Business Review on Measuring Corporate Performance
Harvard Business Review on Mergers and Acquisitions
Harvard Business Review on Motivating People
Harvard Business Review on Negotiation and Conflict Resolution
Harvard Business Review on Nonprofits
Harvard Business Review on Organizational Learning
Harvard Business Review on Strategic Alliances
Harvard Business Review on Strategies for Growth
Harvard Business Review on Turnarounds
Harvard Business Review on Work and Life Balance

Harvard Business Review

ON

TEAMS THAT SUCCEED

A HARVARD BUSINESS REVIEW PAPERBACK

The *Harvard Business Review* articles in this collection are available as
individual reprints. Discounts apply to quantity purchases. For information and ordering, please contact Customer Service, Harvard Business
School Publishing, Boston, MA 02163. Telephone: (617) 783-7500 or
(800) 988-0886, 8 A.M. to 6 P.M. Eastern Time, Monday through Friday.
Fax: (617) 783-7555, 24 hours a day. E-mail: custserv@hbsp.harvard.edu

Library of Congress Cataloging-in-Publication Data
Harvard business review on teams that succeed.
     p.   cm. — (A Harvard business review paperback)
    Includes index.
    ISBN 1-59139-502-X
    1. Teams in the workplace. 2. Employee motivation. 3. Organiza-
tional effectiveness. I. Harvard business review. II. Harvard business
review paperback series.
    HD66.H3766 2004
    658.4'036—dc22   2003022963
                                      CIP

*The paper used in this publication meets the requirements of the Ameri-
can National Standard for Permanence of Paper for Publications and
Documents in Libraries and Archives Z39.48–1992.*

Contents

The Discipline of Teams   1
JON R. KATZENBACH AND DOUGLAS K. SMITH

Building the Emotional Intelligence of Groups   27
VANESSA URCH DRUSKAT AND STEVEN B. WOLFF

Why Bad Projects Are So Hard to Kill   53
ISABELLE ROYER

Speeding Up Team Learning   77
AMY EDMONDSON, RICHARD BOHMER, AND GARY PISANO

What You Don't Know About Making Decisions   99
DAVID A. GARVIN AND MICHAEL A. ROBERTO

Communities of Practice:
The Organizational Frontier   123
ETIENNE C. WENGER AND WILLIAM M. SNYDER

How the Right Measures Help Teams Excel   143
CHRISTOPHER MEYER

The Nut Island Effect:
When Good Teams Go Wrong   167
PAUL F. LEVY

About the Contributors   187

Index   191

The Discipline of Teams

JON R. KATZENBACH AND

DOUGLAS K. SMITH

Executive Summary

GROUPS DON'T BECOME TEAMS because that is what someone calls them. Nor do teamwork values by themselves ensure team performance. So what is a team? How can managers know when the team option makes sense and what they can do to ensure team success? In this article, drawn from their recent book *The Wisdom of Teams,* McKinsey partners Jon Katzenbach and Douglas Smith answer these questions and outline the discipline that makes a real team.

The essence of a team is shared commitment. Without it, groups perform as individuals; with it, they become a powerful unit of collective performance. The best teams invest a tremendous amount of time shaping a purpose that they can own. The best teams also translate their purpose into specific performance goals. And members of successful teams pitch in and become accountable with and to their teammates.

The fundamental distinction between teams and other forms of working groups turns on performance. A working group relies on the individual contributions of its members for group performance. But a team strives for something greater than its members could achieve individually. In short, an effective team is always worth more than the sum of its parts.

Katzenbach and Smith identify three basic types of teams: teams that recommend things—task forces or project groups; teams that make or do things—manufacturing, operations, or marketing groups; and teams that run things—groups that oversee some significant functional activity. For managers, the key is knowing where in the organization real teams should be encouraged. Team potential exists anywhere hierarchy or organizational boundaries inhibit good performance. Considering the extra level that teams can achieve, the authors believe that teams will become the primary work unit in high-performance organizations.

Early in the 1980s, Bill Greenwood and a small band of rebel railroaders took on most of the top management of Burlington Northern and created a multibillion-dollar business in "piggybacking" rail services despite widespread resistance, even resentment, within the company. The Medical Products Group at Hewlett-Packard owes most of its leading performance to the remarkable efforts of Dean Morton, Lew Platt, Ben Holmes, Dick Alberting, and a handful of their colleagues who revitalized a health care business that most others had written off. At Knight-Ridder, Jim Batten's "customer obsession" vision took root at the *Tallahassee Democrat* when 14 frontline enthusiasts turned a charter to eliminate errors into a mission of major change and took the entire paper along with them.

Such are the stories and the work of teams—real teams that perform, not amorphous groups that we call teams because we think that the label is motivating and energizing. The difference between teams that perform and other groups that don't is a subject to which most of us pay far too little attention. Part of the problem is that *team* is a word and concept so familiar to everyone.

Or at least that's what we thought when we set out to do research for our book *The Wisdom of Teams*. We wanted to discover what differentiates various levels of team performance, where and how teams work best, and what top management can do to enhance their effectiveness. We talked with hundreds of people on more than 50 different teams in 30 companies and beyond, from Motorola and Hewlett-Packard to Operation Desert Storm and the Girl Scouts.

We found that there is a basic discipline that makes teams work. We also found that teams and good performance are inseparable; you cannot have one without the other. But people use the word *team* so loosely that it gets in the way of learning and applying the discipline that leads to good performance. For managers to make better decisions about whether, when, or how to encourage and use teams, it is important to be more precise about what a team is and what it isn't.

Most executives advocate teamwork. And they should. Teamwork represents a set of values that encourage listening and responding constructively to views expressed by others, giving others the benefit of the doubt, providing support, and recognizing the interests and achievements of others. Such values help teams perform, and they also promote individual performance as well as the performance of an entire organization. But teamwork values by themselves are not exclusive to teams, nor are they enough to ensure team performance.

Nor is a team just any group working together. Committees, councils, and task forces are not necessarily teams. Groups do not become teams simply because that is what someone calls them. The entire work force of any large and complex organization is *never* a team, but think about how often that platitude is offered up.

To understand how teams deliver extra performance, we must distinguish between teams and other forms of working groups. That distinction turns on performance results. A working group's performance is a function of what its members do as individuals. A team's performance includes both individual results and what we call "collective work-products." A collective work-product is what two or more members must work on together, such as interviews, surveys, or experiments. Whatever it is, a collective work-product reflects the joint, real contribution of team members.

Working groups are both prevalent and effective in large organizations where individual accountability is most important. The best working groups come together to share information, perspectives, and insights; to make decisions that help each person do his or her job better; and to reinforce individual performance standards. But the focus is always on individual goals and accountabilities. Working-group members don't take responsibility for results other than their own. Nor do they try to develop incremental performance contributions requiring the combined work of two or more members.

Teams differ fundamentally from working groups because they require both individual and mutual accountability. Teams rely on more than group discussion, debate, and decision; on more than sharing information and best practice performance standards. Teams produce discrete work-products through the joint contributions of their members. This is what makes possible performance levels greater than the sum of all the individual bests of team members. Simply stated, a team is more than the sum of its parts. See "Not All Groups Are Teams: How to Tell the Difference" for more detail.

The first step in developing a disciplined approach to team management is to think about teams as discrete units of performance and not just as positive sets of values. Having observed and worked with scores of teams in action, both successes and failures, we offer the following. Think of it as a working definition or, better still, an essential discipline that real teams share.

A team is a small number of people with complementary skills who are committed to a common purpose, set of performance goals, and approach for which they hold themselves mutually accountable.

THE ESSENCE OF A TEAM is common commitment. Without it, groups perform as individuals; with it, they become a powerful unit of collective performance. This kind of commitment requires a purpose in which team members can believe. Whether the purpose is to "transform the contributions of suppliers into the satisfaction of customers," to "make our company one we can be proud of again," or to "prove that all children can learn," credible team purposes have an element related to winning, being first, revolutionizing, or being on the cutting edge.

Teams develop direction, momentum, and commitment by working to shape a meaningful purpose. Building ownership and commitment to team purpose, however, is not incompatible with taking initial direction from outside the team. The often-asserted assumption that a team cannot "own" its purpose unless management leaves it alone actually confuses more potential teams than it helps. In fact, it is the exceptional case—for example, entrepreneurial situations—when a team creates a purpose entirely on its own.

Not All Groups Are Teams: How to Tell the Difference

Working Group	Team
• Strong, clearly focused leader	• Shared leadership roles
• Individual accountability	• Individual and mutual accountability
• The group's purpose is the same as the broader organizational mission	• Specific team purpose that the team itself delivers
• Individual work-products	• Collective work-products
• Runs efficient meetings	• Encourages open-ended discussion and active problem-solving meetings
• Measures its effectiveness indirectly by its influence on others (e.g., financial performance of the business)	• Measures performance directly by assessing collective work-products
• Discusses, decides, and delegates	• Discusses, decides, and does real work together

Most successful teams shape their purposes in response to a demand or opportunity put in their path, usually by higher management. This helps teams get started by broadly framing the company's performance expectation. Management is responsible for clarifying the charter, rationale, and performance challenge for the team, but management must also leave enough flexibility for the team to develop commitment around its own spin on that purpose, set of specific goals, timing, and approach.

The best teams invest a tremendous amount of time and effort exploring, shaping, and agreeing on a purpose that belongs to them both collectively and individually. This "purposing" activity continues throughout the life of the team. In contrast, failed teams rarely develop a common purpose. For whatever reason—an insufficient focus on performance, lack of effort, poor leadership— they do not coalesce around a challenging aspiration.

The best teams also translate their common purpose into specific performance goals, such as reducing the reject rate from suppliers by 50% or increasing the math scores of graduates from 40% to 95%. Indeed, if a team fails to establish specific performance goals or if those goals do not relate directly to the team's overall purpose, team members become confused, pull apart, and revert to mediocre performance. By contrast, when purposes and goals build on one another and are combined with team commitment, they become a powerful engine of performance.

Transforming broad directives into specific and measurable performance goals is the surest first step for a team trying to shape a purpose meaningful to its members. Specific goals, such as getting a new product to market in less than half the normal time, responding to all customers within 24 hours, or achieving a zero-defect rate while simultaneously cutting costs by 40%, all provide firm footholds for teams. There are several reasons:

- Specific team performance goals help to define a set of work-products that are different both from an organizationwide mission and from individual job objectives. As a result, such work-products require the collective effort of team members to make something specific happen that, in and of itself, adds real value to results. By contrast, simply gathering from time to time to make decisions will not sustain team performance.

- The specificity of performance objectives facilitates clear communication and constructive conflict within the team. When a plant-level team, for example, sets a goal of reducing average machine changeover time to two hours, the clarity of the goal forces the team to concentrate on what it would take either to achieve or to reconsider the goal. When such goals are clear, discussions can focus on how to pursue them or whether to change them; when goals are ambiguous or nonexistent, such discussions are much less productive.

- The attainability of specific goals helps teams maintain their focus on getting results. A product-development team at Eli Lilly's Peripheral Systems Division set definite yardsticks for the market introduction of an ultrasonic probe to help doctors locate deep veins and arteries. The probe had to have an audible signal through a specified depth of tissue, be capable of being manufactured at a rate of 100 per day, and have a unit cost less than a preestablished amount. Because the team could measure its progress against each of these specific objectives, the team knew throughout the development process where it stood. Either it had achieved its goals or not.

- As Outward Bound and other team-building programs illustrate, specific objectives have a leveling effect conducive to team behavior. When a small group of people challenge themselves to get over a wall or to reduce cycle time by 50%, their respective titles, perks, and other stripes fade into the background. The teams that succeed evaluate what and how each individual can best contribute to the team's goal and, more important, do so in terms of the performance objective itself rather than a person's status or personality.

- Specific goals allow a team to achieve small wins as it pursues its broader purpose. These small wins are invaluable to building commitment and overcoming the inevitable obstacles that get in the way of a long-term purpose. For example, the Knight-Ridder team mentioned at the outset turned a narrow goal to eliminate errors into a compelling customer-service purpose.

- Performance goals are compelling. They are symbols of accomplishment that motivate and energize. They challenge the people on a team to commit themselves, as a team, to make a difference. Drama, urgency, and a healthy fear of failure combine to drive teams who have their collective eye on an attainable, but challenging, goal. Nobody but the team can make it happen. It is their challenge.

The combination of purpose and specific goals is essential to performance. Each depends on the other to

remain relevant and vital. Clear performance goals help a
team keep track of progress and hold itself accountable;
the broader, even nobler, aspirations in a team's purpose
supply both meaning and emotional energy.

V IRTUALLY ALL EFFECTIVE TEAMS we have met,
read or heard about, or been members of have ranged
between 2 and 25 people. For example, the Burlington
Northern "piggybacking" team had 7 members, the
Knight-Ridder newspaper team, 14. The majority of them
have numbered less than 10. Small size is admittedly
more of a pragmatic guide than an absolute necessity for
success. A large number of people, say 50 or more, can
theoretically become a team. But groups of such size are
more likely to break into subteams rather than function
as a single unit.

Why? Large numbers of people have trouble interact-
ing constructively as a group, much less doing real work
together. Ten people are far more likely than fifty are to
work through their individual, functional, and hierarchical differences toward a common plan and to hold themselves jointly accountable for the results.

Large groups also face logistical issues, such as finding enough physical space and time to meet. And they
confront more complex constraints, like crowd or herd
behaviors, which prevent the intense sharing of viewpoints needed to build a team. As a result, when they try
to develop a common purpose, they usually produce only
superficial "missions" and well-meaning intentions that
cannot be translated into concrete objectives. They tend
fairly quickly to reach a point when meetings become a
chore, a clear sign that most of the people in the group
are uncertain why they have gathered, beyond some

notion of getting along better. Anyone who has been through one of these exercises knows how frustrating it can be. This kind of failure tends to foster cynicism, which gets in the way of future team efforts.

In addition to finding the right size, teams must develop the right mix of skills, that is, each of the complementary skills necessary to do the team's job. As obvious as it sounds, it is a common failing in potential teams. Skill requirements fall into three fairly self-evident categories:

Technical or functional expertise. It would make little sense for a group of doctors to litigate an employment discrimination case in a court of law. Yet teams of doctors and lawyers often try medical malpractice or personal injury cases. Similarly, product-development groups that include only marketers or engineers are less likely to succeed than those with the complementary skills of both.

Problem-solving and decision-making skills. Teams must be able to identify the problems and opportunities they face, evaluate the options they have for moving forward, and then make necessary trade-offs and decisions about how to proceed. Most teams need some members with these skills to begin with, although many will develop them best on the job.

Interpersonal skills. Common understanding and purpose cannot arise without effective communication and constructive conflict, which in turn depend on interpersonal skills. These include risk taking, helpful criticism, objectivity, active listening, giving the benefit of the doubt, and recognizing the interests and achievements of others.

Obviously, a team cannot get started without some minimum complement of skills, especially technical and functional ones. Still, think about how often you've been part of a team whose members were chosen primarily on the basis of personal compatibility or formal position in the organization, and in which the skill mix of its members wasn't given much thought.

It is equally common to overemphasize skills in team selection. Yet in all the successful teams we've encountered, not one had all the needed skills at the outset. The Burlington Northern team, for example, initially had no members who were skilled marketers despite the fact that their performance challenge was a marketing one. In fact, we discovered that teams are powerful vehicles for developing the skills needed to meet the team's performance challenge. Accordingly, team member selection ought to ride as much on skill potential as on skills already proven.

EFFECTIVE TEAMS DEVELOP strong commitment to a common approach, that is, to how they will work together to accomplish their purpose. Team members must agree on who will do particular jobs, how schedules will be set and adhered to, what skills need to be developed, how continuing membership in the team is to be earned, and how the group will make and modify decisions. This element of commitment is as important to team performance as is the team's commitment to its purpose and goals.

Agreeing on the specifics of work and how they fit together to integrate individual skills and advance team performance lies at the heart of shaping a common approach. It is perhaps self-evident that an approach that delegates all the real work to a few members (or staff outsiders), and thus relies on reviews and meetings for its only "work together" aspects, cannot sustain a real team. Every member of a successful team does equivalent amounts of real work; all members, including the team leader, contribute in concrete ways to the team's work-product. This is a very important element of the emotional logic that drives team performance.

When individuals approach a team situation, especially in a business setting, each has preexisting job assignments as well as strengths and weaknesses reflecting a variety of backgrounds, talents, personalities, and prejudices. Only through the mutual discovery and understanding of how to apply all its human resources to a common purpose can a team develop and agree on the best approach to achieve its goals. At the heart of such long and, at times, difficult interactions lies a commitment-building process in which the team candidly explores who is best suited to each task as well as how individual roles will come together. In effect, the team establishes a social contract among members that relates to their purpose and guides and obligates how they must work together.

No group ever becomes a team until it can hold itself accountable as a team. Like common purpose and approach, mutual accountability is a stiff test. Think, for example, about the subtle but critical difference between "the boss holds me accountable" and "we hold ourselves accountable." The first case can lead to the second; but without the second, there can be no team.

Companies like Hewlett-Packard and Motorola have an ingrained performance ethic that enables teams to form "organically" whenever there is a clear performance challenge requiring collective rather than individual

effort. In these companies, the factor of mutual accountability is commonplace. "Being in the boat together" is
how their performance game is played.

At its core, team accountability is about the sincere
promises we make to ourselves and others, promises that
underpin two critical aspects of effective teams: commitment and trust. Most of us enter a potential team situation cautiously because ingrained individualism and
experience discourage us from putting our fates in the
hands of others or accepting responsibility for others.
Teams do not succeed by ignoring or wishing away such
behavior.

Mutual accountability cannot be coerced any more
than people can be made to trust one another. But when
a team shares a common purpose, goals, and approach,
mutual accountability grows as a natural counterpart.
Accountability arises from and reinforces the time,
energy, and action invested in figuring out what the team
is trying to accomplish and how best to get it done.

When people work together toward a common objective, trust and commitment follow. Consequently, teams
enjoying a strong common purpose and approach
inevitably hold themselves responsible, both as individuals and as a team, for the team's performance. This sense
of mutual accountability also produces the rich rewards
of mutual achievement in which all members share.
What we heard over and over from members of effective
teams is that they found the experience energizing and
motivating in ways that their "normal" jobs never could
match.

On the other hand, groups established primarily for
the sake of becoming a team or for job enhancement,
communication, organizational effectiveness, or excellence rarely become effective teams, as demonstrated by

the bad feelings left in many companies after experimenting with quality circles that never translated "quality" into specific goals. Only when appropriate performance goals are set does the process of discussing the goals and the approaches to them give team members a clearer and clearer choice: they can disagree with a goal and the path that the team selects and, in effect, opt out, or they can pitch in and become accountable with and to their teammates.

THE DISCIPLINE OF TEAMS we've outlined is critical to the success of all teams. Yet it is also useful to go one step further. Most teams can be classified in one of three ways: teams that recommend things, teams that make or do things, and teams that run things. In our experience, each type faces a characteristic set of challenges.

Teams That Recommend Things

These teams include task forces, project groups, and audit, quality, or safety groups asked to study and solve particular problems. Teams that recommend things almost always have predetermined completion dates. Two critical issues are unique to such teams: getting off to a fast and constructive start and dealing with the ultimate handoff required to get recommendations implemented.

The key to the first issue lies in the clarity of the team's charter and the composition of its membership. In addition to wanting to know why and how their efforts are important, task forces need a clear definition of whom management expects to participate and the time commitment required. Management can help by ensuring that the team includes people with the skills and influence necessary for crafting practical recommendations that will carry weight throughout the organization. Moreover, management can help the team get the necessary cooperation by opening doors and dealing with political obstacles.

Missing the handoff is almost always the problem that stymies teams that recommend things. To avoid this, the transfer of responsibility for recommendations to those who must implement them demands top management's time and attention. The more top managers assume that recommendations will "just happen," the less likely it is that they will. The more involvement task force members have in implementing their recommendations, the more likely they are to get implemented.

To the extent that people outside the task force will have to carry the ball, it is critical to involve them in the process early and often, certainly well before recommendations are finalized. Such involvement may take many forms, including participating in interviews, helping with analyses, contributing and critiquing ideas, and conducting experiments and trials. At a minimum, anyone responsible for implementation should receive a briefing on the task force's purpose, approach, and objectives at the beginning of the effort as well as regular reviews of progress.

Teams That Make or Do Things

These teams include people at or near the front lines who are responsible for doing the basic manufacturing, development, operations, marketing, sales, service, and other value-adding activities of a business. With some exceptions, like new-product development or process design teams, teams that make or do things tend to have no set completion dates because their activities are ongoing.

In deciding where team performance might have the greatest impact, top management should concentrate on what we call the company's "critical delivery points," that is, places in the organization where the cost and value of the company's products and services are most directly determined. Such critical delivery points might include where accounts get managed, customer service performed, products designed, and productivity determined. If performance at critical delivery points depends on combining multiple skills, perspectives, and judgments in real time, then the team option is the smartest one.

When an organization does require a significant number of teams at these points, the sheer challenge of maximizing the performance of so many groups will demand a carefully constructed and performance-focused set of management processes. The issue here for top management is how to build the necessary systems and process supports without falling into the trap of appearing to promote teams for their own sake.

The imperative here, returning to our earlier discussion of the basic discipline of teams, is a relentless focus on performance. If management fails to pay persistent attention to the link between teams and performance, the organization becomes convinced that "this year we are doing 'teams.'" Top management can help by instituting processes like pay schemes and training for teams responsive to their real time needs, but more than anything else, top management must make clear and compelling demands on the teams themselves and then pay constant attention to their progress with respect to both team basics and performance results. This means focusing on specific teams and specific performance challenges. Otherwise "performance," like "team," will become a cliché.

Teams That Run Things

Despite the fact that many leaders refer to the group reporting to them as a team, few groups really are. And groups that become real teams seldom think of themselves as a team because they are so focused on performance results. Yet the opportunity for such teams includes groups from the top of the enterprise down through the divisional or functional level. Whether it is in charge of thousands of people or a handful, as long as the group oversees some business, ongoing program, or significant functional activity, it is a team that runs things.

The main issue these teams face is determining whether a real team approach is the right one. Many groups that run things can be more effective as working groups than as teams. The key judgment is whether the sum of individual bests will suffice for the performance challenge at hand or whether the group must deliver substantial incremental performance requiring real, joint work-products. Although the team option promises greater performance, it also brings more risk, and managers must be brutally honest in assessing the trade-offs.

Members may have to overcome a natural reluctance to trust their fate to others. The price of faking the team approach is high: at best, members get diverted from their individual goals, costs outweigh benefits, and people resent the imposition on their time and priorities; at worst, serious animosities develop that undercut even the potential personal bests of the working-group approach.

Working groups present fewer risks. Effective working groups need little time to shape their purpose since the leader usually establishes it. Meetings are run against well-prioritized agendas. And decisions are implemented through specific individual assignments and account-abilities. Most of the time, therefore, if performance aspirations can be met through individuals doing their respective jobs well, the working-group approach is more comfortable, less risky, and less disruptive than trying for more elusive team performance levels. Indeed, if there is no performance need for the team approach, efforts spent to improve the effectiveness of the working group make much more sense than floundering around trying to become a team.

Having said that, we believe the extra level of performance teams can achieve is becoming critical for a growing number of companies, especially as they move through major changes during which company performance depends on broad-based behavioral change. When top management uses teams to run things, it should make sure the team succeeds in identi-fying specific purposes and goals.

This is a second major issue for teams that run things. Too often, such teams confuse the broad mission of the total organization with the specific purpose of their small group at the top. The discipline of teams tells us that for a real team to form there must be a *team* pur-pose that is distinctive and specific to the small group and that requires its members to roll up their sleeves and accomplish something beyond individual end-products. If a group of managers looks only at the economic performance of the part of the organization it runs to assess overall effectiveness, the group will not have any team performance goals of its own.

While the basic discipline of teams does not differ for them, teams at the top are certainly the most difficult. The complexities of long-term challenges, heavy demands on executive time, and the deep-seated individualism of senior people conspire against teams at the top. At the same time, teams at the top are the most powerful. At first we thought such teams were nearly impossible. That is because we were looking at the teams as defined by the formal organizational structure, that is, the leader and all his or her direct reports equals the team. Then we discovered that real teams at the top were often smaller and less formalized—Whitehead and Weinberg at Goldman, Sachs; Hewlett and Packard at HP; Krasnoff, Pall, and Hardy at Pall Corp; Kendall, Pearson, and Calloway at Pepsi; Haas and Haas at Levi Strauss; Batten and Ridder at Knight-Ridder. They were mostly twos and threes, with an occasional fourth.

Nonetheless, real teams at the top of large, complex organizations are still few and far between. Far too many groups at the top of large corporations needlessly constrain themselves from achieving real team levels of performance because they assume that all direct reports must be on the team; that team goals must be identical to corporate goals; that the team members' positions rather than skills determine their respective roles; that a team must be a team all the time; and that the team leader is above doing real work.

As understandable as these assumptions may be, most of them are unwarranted. They do not apply to the teams at the top we have observed, and when replaced with more realistic and flexible assumptions that permit the team discipline to be applied, real team performance at the top can and does occur. Moreover, as more and more companies are confronted with the need to manage major change across their organizations, we will see more real teams at the top.

W E BELIEVE THAT TEAMS will become the primary unit of performance in high-performance organizations. But that does not mean that teams will crowd out individual opportunity or formal hierarchy and process. Rather, teams will enhance existing structures without replacing them. A team opportunity exists anywhere hierarchy or organizational boundaries inhibit the skills and perspectives needed for optimal results. Thus, new-product innovation requires preserving functional excellence through structure while eradicating functional bias through teams. And frontline productivity requires preserving direction and guidance through hierarchy while drawing on energy and flexibility through self-managing teams.

We are convinced that every company faces specific performance challenges for which teams are the most practical and powerful vehicle at top management's disposal. The critical role for senior managers, therefore, is to worry about company performance and the kinds of teams that can deliver it. This means that top management must recognize a team's unique potential to deliver results, deploy teams strategically when they are the best tool for the job, and foster the basic discipline of teams that will make them effective. By doing so, top management creates the kind of environment that enables team as well as individual and organizational performance.

Building Team Performance

ALTHOUGH THERE IS NO guaranteed how-to recipe for building team performance, we observed a number of approaches shared by many successful teams.

Establish urgency, demanding performance standards, and direction

All team members need to believe the team has urgent and worthwhile purposes, and they want to know what the expectations are. Indeed, the more urgent and meaningful the rationale, the more likely it is that the team will live up to its performance potential, as was the case for a customer-service team that was told that further growth for the entire company would be impossible without major improvements in that area. Teams work best in a compelling context. That is why companies with strong performance ethics usually form teams readily.

Select members for skill and skill potential, not personality

No team succeeds without all the skills needed to meet its purpose and performance goals. Yet most teams figure out the skills they will need after they are formed. The wise manager will choose people both for their existing skills and their potential to improve existing skills and learn new ones.

Pay particular attention to first meetings and actions

Initial impressions always mean a great deal. When potential teams first gather, everyone monitors the signals given by others to confirm, suspend, or dispel assumptions and concerns. They pay particular attention to those in authority: the team leader and any executives who set up, oversee, or otherwise influence the team. And, as always, what such leaders do is more important than what they say. If a senior executive leaves the team kick-off to take a phone call ten minutes after the session has begun and he never returns, people get the message.

Set some clear rules of behavior

All effective teams develop rules of conduct at the outset to help them achieve their purpose and performance goals. The most critical initial rules pertain to attendance (for example, "no interruptions to take phone calls"), discussion ("no sacred cows"), confidentiality ("the only things to leave this room are what we agree on"), analytic approach ("facts are friendly"), end-product orientation ("everyone gets assignments and does them"), constructive confrontation ("no finger pointing"), and, often the most important, contributions ("everyone does real work").

Set and seize upon a few immediate performance-oriented tasks and goals

Most effective teams trace their advancement to key performance-oriented events. Such events can be set in motion by immediately establishing a few challenging goals that can be reached early on. There is no such thing as a real team without performance results, so the sooner such results occur, the sooner the team congeals.

Challenge the group regularly with fresh facts and information

New information causes a team to redefine and enrich its understanding of the performance challenge, thereby helping the team shape a common purpose, set clearer

goals, and improve its common approach. A plant quality improvement team knew the cost of poor quality was
high, but it wasn't until they researched the different types
of defects and put a price tag on each one that they
knew where to go next. Conversely, teams err when they
assume that all the information needed exists in the collective experience and knowledge of their members.

Spend lots of time together

Common sense tells us that team members must spend a
lot of time together, scheduled and unscheduled, especially in the beginning. Indeed, creative insights as well
as personal bonding require impromptu and casual interactions just as much as analyzing spreadsheets and inter-
viewing customers. Busy executives and managers too
often intentionally minimize the time they spend together.
The successful teams we've observed all gave themselves the time to learn to be a team. This time need not
always be spent together physically; electronic, fax, and
phone time can also count as time spent together.

Exploit the power of positive feedback, recognition, and reward

Positive reinforcement works as well in a team context as
elsewhere. "Giving out gold stars" helps to shape new
behaviors critical to team performance. If people in the
group, for example, are alert to a shy person's initial
efforts to speak up and contribute, they can give the honest positive reinforcement that encourages continued
contributions. There are many ways to recognize and
reward team performance beyond direct compensation,
from having a senior executive speak directly to the team
about the urgency of its mission to using awards to rec-

ognize contributions. Ultimately, however, the satisfaction shared by a team in its own performance becomes the most cherished reward.

Originally published in March 1993
Reprint 93207

Building the Emotional Intelligence of Groups

VANESSA URCH DRUSKAT AND

STEVEN B. WOLFF

Executive Summary

THE MANAGEMENT WORLD KNOWS by now that to be effective in the workplace, an individual needs high emotional intelligence. What isn't so well understood is that teams need it, too.

Citing such companies as IDEO, Hewlett-Packard, and the Hay Group, the authors show that high emotional intelligence is at the heart of effective teams. These teams behave in ways that build relationships both inside and outside the team and that strengthen their ability to face challenges.

High group emotional intelligence may seem like a simple matter of putting a group of emotionally intelligent individuals together. It's not. For a team to have high EI, it needs to create norms that establish mutual trust among members, a sense of group identity, and a sense of group efficacy. These three conditions are essential to a

27

team's effectiveness because they are the foundation of true cooperation and collaboration.

Group EI isn't a question of dealing with a necessary evil—catching emotions as they bubble up and promptly suppressing them. It's about bringing emotions deliberately to the surface and understanding how they affect the team's work. Group emotional intelligence is about exploring, embracing, and ultimately relying on the emotions that are at the core of teams.

WHEN MANAGERS FIRST STARTED hearing about the concept of emotional intelligence in the 1990s, scales fell from their eyes. The basic message, that effectiveness in organizations is at least as much about EQ as IQ, resonated deeply; it was something that people knew in their guts but that had never before been so well articulated. Most important, the idea held the potential for positive change. Instead of being stuck with the hand they'd been dealt, people could take steps to enhance their emotional intelligence and make themselves more effective in their work and personal lives.

Indeed, the concept of emotional intelligence had real impact. The only problem is that so far emotional intelligence has been viewed only as an individual competency, when the reality is that most work in organizations is done by teams. And if managers have one pressing need today, it's to find ways to make teams work better.

It is with real excitement, therefore, that we share these findings from our research: individual emotional intelligence has a group analog, and it is just as critical to groups' effectiveness. Teams can develop greater emotional intelligence and, in so doing, boost their overall performance.

Why Should Teams Build Their Emotional Intelligence?

No one would dispute the importance of making teams work more effectively. But most research about how to do so has focused on identifying the task processes that distinguish the most successful teams—that is, specifying the need for cooperation, participation, commitment to goals, and so forth. The assumption seems to be that, once identified, these processes can simply be imitated by other teams, with similar effect. It's not true. By analogy, think of it this way: a piano student can be taught to play Minuet in G, but he won't become a modern-day Bach without knowing music theory and being able to play with heart. Similarly, the real source of a great team's success lies in the fundamental conditions that allow effective task processes to emerge—and that cause members to engage in them wholeheartedly.

Our research tells us that three conditions are essential to a group's effectiveness: trust among members, a sense of group identity, and a sense of group efficacy. When these conditions are absent, going through the motions of cooperating and participating is still possible. But the team will not be as effective as it could be, because members will choose to hold back rather than fully engage. To be most effective, the team needs to create emotionally intelligent norms—the attitudes and behaviors that eventually become habits—that support behaviors for building trust, group identity, and group efficacy. The outcome is complete engagement in tasks.

(For more on how emotional intelligence influences these conditions, see the exhibit "A Model of Team Effectiveness.")

Three Levels of Emotional Interaction

Make no mistake: a team with emotionally intelligent members does not necessarily make for an emotionally intelligent group. A team, like any social group, takes on its own character. So creating an upward, self-reinforcing spiral of trust, group identity, and group efficacy requires more than a few members who exhibit emotionally intelligent behavior. It requires a team atmosphere in which the norms build emotional capacity (the ability to respond constructively in emotionally uncomfortable situations) and influence emotions in constructive ways.

Team emotional intelligence is more complicated than individual emotional intelligence because teams interact at more levels. To understand the differences, let's first look at the concept of individual emotional intelligence as defined by Daniel Goleman. In his definitive book *Emotional Intelligence*, Goleman explains the chief characteristics of someone with high EI; he or she is *aware* of emotions and able to *regulate* them—and this awareness and regulation are directed both *inward*, to one's self, and *outward*, to others. "Personal competence," in Goleman's words, comes from being aware of and regulating one's own emotions. "Social competence" is awareness and regulation of others' emotions.

A group, however, must attend to yet another level of awareness and regulation. It must be mindful of the emotions of its members, its own group emotions or moods, and the emotions of other groups and individuals outside its boundaries.

A Model of Team Effectiveness

Study after study has shown that teams are more creative and productive when they can achieve high levels of participation, cooperation, and collaboration among members. But interactive behaviors like these aren't easy to legislate. Our work shows that three basic conditions need to be present before such behaviors can occur: mutual trust among members, a sense of group identity (a feeling among members that they belong to a unique and worthwhile group), and a sense of group efficacy (the belief that the team can perform well and that group members are more effective working together than apart).

At the heart of these three conditions are emotions. Trust, a sense of identity, and a feeling of efficacy arise in environments where emotion is well handled, so groups stand to benefit by building their emotional intelligence.

Group emotional intelligence isn't a question of dealing with a necessary evil—catching emotions as they bubble up and promptly suppressing them. Far from it. It's about bringing emotions deliberately to the surface and understanding how they affect the team's work. It's also about behaving in ways that build relationships both inside and outside the team and that strengthen the team's ability to face challenges. Emotional intelligence means exploring, embracing, and ultimately relying on emotion in work that is, at the end of the day, deeply human.

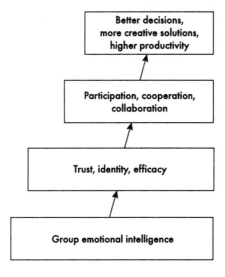

In this article, we'll explore how emotional incompetence at any of these levels can cause dysfunction. We'll also show how establishing specific group norms that create awareness and regulation of emotion at these three levels can lead to better outcomes. First, we'll focus on the individual level—how emotionally intelligent groups work with their individual members' emotions. Next, we'll focus on the group level. And finally, we'll look at the cross-boundary level.

Working with Individuals' Emotions

Jill Kasper, head of her company's customer service department, is naturally tapped to join a new cross-functional team focused on enhancing the customer experience: she has extensive experience in and a real passion for customer service. But her teammates find she brings little more than a bad attitude to the table. At an early brainstorming session, Jill sits silent, arms crossed, rolling her eyes. Whenever the team starts to get energized about an idea, she launches into a detailed account of how a similar idea went nowhere in the past. The group is confused: this is the customer service star they've been hearing about? Little do they realize she feels insulted by the very formation of the team. To her, it implies she hasn't done her job well enough.

When a member is not on the same emotional wavelength as the rest, a team needs to be emotionally intelligent vis-à-vis that individual. In part, that simply means being aware of the problem. Having a norm that encourages interpersonal understanding might facilitate an awareness that Jill is acting out of defensiveness. And picking up on this defensiveness is necessary if the team wants to make her understand its desire to amplify her good work, not negate it.

Some teams seem to be able to do this naturally. At Hewlett-Packard, for instance, we learned of a team that was attempting to cross-train its members. The idea was that if each member could pinch-hit on every-one else's job, the team could deploy efforts to whatever task required the most attention. But one member seemed very uncomfortable with learning new skills and tasks; accustomed to being a top producer in his own job, he hated not knowing how to do a job per-fectly. Luckily, his teammates recognized his discom-fort, and rather than being annoyed, they redoubled their efforts to support him. This team benefited from a group norm it had established over time emphasizing interpersonal understanding. The norm had grown out of the group's realization that working to accurately hear and understand one another's feelings and con-cerns improved member morale and a willingness to cooperate.

Many teams build high emotional intelligence by tak-ing pains to consider matters from an individual mem-ber's perspective. Think of a situation where a team of four must reach a decision; three favor one direction and the fourth favors another. In the interest of expedience, many teams in this situation would move directly to a majority vote. But a more emotionally intelligent group would pause first to hear out the objection. It would also ask if everyone were completely behind the decision, even if there appeared to be consensus. Such groups would ask, "Are there any perspectives we haven't heard yet or thought through completely?"

Perspective taking is a team behavior that teamwork experts discuss often—but not in terms of its emotional consequence. Many teams are trained to use perspective-taking techniques to make decisions or solve problems (a common tool is affinity diagramming). But these techniques may or may not improve a group's emotional intelligence. The problem is that many of these techniques consciously attempt to remove emotion from the process by collecting and combining perspectives in a mechanical way. A more effective approach to perspective taking is to ensure that team members see one another making the effort to grapple with perspectives; that way, the team has a better chance of creating the kind of trust that leads to greater participation among members.

An executive team at the Hay Group, a consulting firm, engages in the kind of deep perspective taking we're describing. The team has done role-playing exercises in which members adopt others' opinions and styles of interaction. It has also used a "storyboarding" technique, in which each member creates a small poster representing his or her ideas. As team members will attest, these methods and others have helped the group build trust and increase participation.

Regulating Individuals' Emotions

Interpersonal understanding and perspective taking are two ways that groups can become more aware of their members' perspectives and feelings. But just as important as awareness is the ability to regulate those emotions—to have a positive impact on how they are expressed and even on how individual team members feel. We're not talking about imposing groupthink or some other form of manipulation here—clearly, the goal must be to balance the team's cohesion with members' individuality. We're simply acknowledging that people take their emotional cues from those around them. Something that seems upsetting initially can seem not so bad—or ten times worse—depending on whether one's colleagues are inclined to smooth feathers or fan flames. The most constructive way of regulating team members' emotions is by establishing norms in the group for both confrontation and caring.

It may seem illogical to suggest that an emotionally intelligent group must engage in confrontation, but it's not. Inevitably, a team member will indulge in behavior that crosses the line, and the team must feel comfortable calling the foul. In one manufacturing team we studied, a member told us about the day she selfishly decided to extend her break. Before long, one of her teammates stormed into the break room, saying, "What are you doing in here? Get back out on the floor—your team needs you!" The woman had overstepped the bounds, and she got called on it. There were no hard feelings, because the woman knew the group valued her contributions.

Some teams also find that a little humor helps when pointing out errant behavior. Teasing someone who is habitually late for meetings, for instance, can make that person aware of how important timeliness is to the group. Done right, confrontation can be seen in a positive light; it's a way for the group to say, "We want you in—we need your contribution." And it's especially important when a team must work together on a long-term assignment. Without confrontation, disruptive behavior can fester and erode a sense of trust in a team.

Establishing norms that reinforce caring behavior is often not very difficult and usually a matter of concentrating on little things. When an individual is upset, for example, it may make all the difference to have group members acknowledge that person's feelings. We saw this in a meeting where one team member arrived angry because the time and place of the meeting was very inconvenient for him. When another member announced the sacrifice the man had made to be there, and thanked him, the man's attitude turned around 180 degrees. In general, a caring orientation includes displaying positive regard, appreciation, and respect for group members through behaviors such as support, validation, and compassion.

Interpersonal understanding, perspective taking, confrontation, caring—these norms build trust and a sense of group identity among members. And all of them can be established in teams where they don't arise naturally. You may ask, But is it really worth all the effort? Does it make sense to spend managerial time fostering new norms to accommodate a few prickly personalities? Of course it does. Teams are at the very foundation of an organization, and they won't work effectively without mutual trust and a common commitment to goals.

Working with Group Emotions

Chris couldn't believe it, but he was requesting a reassignment. The team he was on was doing good work, staying on budget, and hitting all its deadlines—though not always elegantly. Its leader, Stan Evans, just got a promotion. So why was being on the team such a downer? At the last major status meeting, they should have been serving champagne—so much had been achieved. Instead, everyone was thoroughly dispirited over a setback they hadn't foreseen, which turned out later to be no big deal. It seemed no matter what happened, the group griped. The team even saw Stan's promotion in a negative light: "Oh, so I guess management wants to keep a closer eye on us" and "I hear Stan's new boss doesn't back this project." Chris had a friend on another team who was happy to put in a good word for him. The work was inherently less interesting—but hey, at least they were having fun.

Some teams suffer because they aren't aware of emotions at the group level. Chris's team, for instance, isn't aware of all it has achieved, and it doesn't acknowledge that it has fallen into a malaise. In our study of effective teams, we've found that having norms for group self-awareness—of emotional states, strengths and weaknesses, modes of interaction, and task processes—is a critical part of group emotional intelligence that facilitates group efficacy. Teams gain it both through self-evaluation and by soliciting feedback from others.

Self-evaluation can take the form of a formal event or a constant activity. At Sherwin Williams, a group of managers was starting a new initiative that would require higher levels of teamwork. Group members hired a consultant, but before the consultant arrived, they met to assess their strengths and weaknesses as a team. They found that merely articulating the issues was an important step toward building their capabilities.

A far less formal method of raising group emotional awareness is through the kind of activity we saw at the Veterans Health Administration's Center for Leadership and Development. Managers there have developed a norm in which they are encouraged to speak up when they feel the group is not being productive. For example, if there's a post-lunch lull and people on the team are low on energy, someone might say, "Don't we look like a

bunch of sad sacks?" With attention called to it, the
group makes an effort to refocus.

Emotionally competent teams don't wear blinders;
they have the emotional capacity to face potentially difficult information and actively seek opinions on their task
processes, progress, and performance from the outside.
For some teams, feedback may come directly from customers. Others look to colleagues within the company, to
suppliers, or to professional peers. A group of designers
we studied routinely posts its work in progress on walls
throughout the building, with invitations to comment
and critique. Similarly, many advertising agencies see
annual industry competitions as a valuable source of
feedback on their creative teams' work.

Regulating Group Emotions

Many teams make conscious efforts to build team spirit.
Team-building outings, whether purely social or Outward Bound–style physical challenges, are popular
methods for building this sense of collective enthusiasm.
What's going on here is that teams and their leaders recognize they can improve a team's overall attitude—that
is, they are regulating group-level emotion. And while
the focus of a team-building exercise is often not directly
related to a group's actual work, the benefits are highly
relevant: teams come away with higher emotional capacity and thus a greater ability to respond to emotional
challenges.

The most effective teams we have studied go far
beyond the occasional "ropes and rocks" off-site. They
have established norms that strengthen their ability to
respond effectively to the kind of emotional challenges a
group confronts on a daily basis. The norms they favor

accomplish three main things: they create resources for working with emotions, foster an affirmative environment, and encourage proactive problem solving.

Teams need resources that all members can draw on to deal with group emotions. One important resource is a common vocabulary. To use an example, a group member at the Veterans Health Administration picked up on another member's bad mood and told him that he was just "cranky" today. The "cranky" term stuck and became the group's gentle way of letting someone know that their negativity was having a bad effect on the group. Other resources may include helpful ways to vent frustrations. One executive team leader we interviewed described his team's practice of making time for a "wailing wall"—a few minutes of whining and moaning about some setback. Releasing and acknowledging those negative emotions, the leader says, allows the group to refocus its attention on the parts of the situation it can control and channel its energy in a positive direction. But sometimes, venting takes more than words. We've seen more than one intense workplace outfitted with toys—like soft projectile shooters—that have been used in games of cube warfare.

Perhaps the most obvious way to build emotional capacity through regulating team-level emotion is simply to create an affirmative environment. Everyone values a team that, when faced with a challenge, responds with a can-do attitude. Again, it's a question of having the right group norms—in this case, favoring optimism, and positive images and interpretations over negative ones. This doesn't always come naturally to a team, as one executive we interviewed at the Hay Group knows. When external conditions create a cycle of negativity among group members, he takes it upon himself to change the atmosphere of the group. He consciously resists the temptation to join the complaining and blaming and instead tries to reverse the cycle with a positive, constructive note.

One of the most powerful norms we have seen for building a group's ability to respond to emotionally challenging situations is an emphasis on proactive problem solving. We saw a lot of this going on in a manufacturing team we observed at AMP Corporation. Much of what this team needed to hit its targets was out of its strict control. But rather than sit back and point fingers, the team worked hard to get what it needed from others, and in some cases, took matters into its own hands. In one instance, an alignment problem in a key machine was creating faulty products. The team studied the problem and approached the engineering group with its own suggested design for a part that might correct the problem. The device worked, and the number of defective products decreased significantly.

This kind of problem solving is valuable for many reasons. It obviously serves the company by removing one more obstacle to profitability. But, to the point of our work, it also shows a team in control of its own emotions. It refused to feel powerless and was eager to take charge.

Working with Emotions Outside the Group

Jim sighed. The "Bugs" team was at it again. Didn't they see that while they were high-fiving one another over their impressive productivity, the rest of the organization was paying for it? This time, in their self-managed wisdom, they'd decided to make a three months' supply of one component. No changeover meant no machine downtime and a record low cost per unit. But now the group downstream was swamped with inventory it didn't need and worried about shortages of something else. Jim braced himself for his visit to the floor. The Bugs didn't take criticism well; they seemed to think they were flawless and that everyone else was just trying to take them down a notch. And what was with that name, anyway? Some kind of inside joke, Jim guessed. Too bad nobody else got it.

The last kind of emotional intelligence any high-performing team should have relates to cross-boundary relationships. Just as individuals should be mindful of their own emotions and others', groups should look both inward and outward emotionally. In the case of the Bugs, the team is acting like a clique—creating close emotional ties within but ignoring the feelings, needs, and concerns of important individuals and teams in the broader organization.

Some teams have developed norms that are particularly helpful in making them aware of the broader organizational context. One practice is to have various team members act as liaisons to important constituencies. Many teams are already made up of members drawn from different parts of an organization, so a cross-boundary perspective comes naturally. Others need to work a little harder. One team we studied realized it would be important to understand the perspective of its labor union. Consequently, a team member from HR went to some lengths to discover the right channels for having a union member appointed to the group. A cross-boundary perspective is especially important in situations where a team's work will have significant impact on others in the organization—for example, where a team is asked to design an intranet to serve everyone's needs. We've seen many situations in which a team is so enamored of its solution that it is caught completely by surprise when others in the company don't share its enthusiasm.

Some of the most emotionally intelligent teams we have seen are so attuned to their broader organizational context that it affects how they frame and communicate their own needs and accomplishments. A team at the chemical-processing company KoSa, for example, felt it needed a new piece of manufacturing equipment, but senior management wasn't so sure the purchase was a priority. Aware that the decision makers were still on the fence, the team decided to emphasize the employee safety benefits of the new machine—just one aspect of its desirability to them, but an issue of paramount importance to management. At a plant safety meeting attended by high-level managers, they made the case that the equipment they were seeking would greatly reduce the risk of injury to workers. A few weeks later they got it.

Sometimes, a team must be particularly aware of the needs and feelings of another group within the organization. We worked with an information technology company where the hardware engineers worked separately from the software engineers to achieve the same goal—faster processing and fewer crashes. Each could achieve only so much independently. When finally a hardware team leader went out of his way to build relationships with the software people, the two teams began to cooperate—and together, they achieved 20% to 40% higher performance than had been targeted.

This kind of positive outcome can be facilitated by norms that encourage a group to recognize the feelings and needs of other groups. We saw effective norms for interteam awareness at a division of AMP, where each manufacturing team is responsible for a step in the manufacturing process and they need one another to complete the product on time. Team leaders there meet in the morning to understand the needs, resources, and schedules of each team. If one team is ahead and another is behind, they reallocate resources. Members of the faster team help the team that's behind and do so in a friendly way that empathizes with their situation and builds the relationship.

Most of the examples we've been citing show teams that are not only aware of but also able to influence outsiders' needs and perspectives. This ability to regulate emotion at the cross-boundary level is a group's version of the "social skills" so critical to individual emotional intelligence. It involves developing external relationships and gaining the confidence of outsiders, adopting an ambassadorial role instead of an isolationist one.

A manufacturing team we saw at KoSa displayed very high social skills in working with its maintenance team. It recognized that, when problems occurred in the plant, the maintenance team often had many activities on its plate. All things being equal, what would make the maintenance team consider this particular manufacturing group a high priority? Knowing a good relationship would be a factor, the manufacturing team worked hard to build good ties with the maintenance people. At one point, for instance, the manufacturing team showed its appreciation by nominating the maintenance team for "Team of the Quarter" recognition—and then doing all the letter writing and behind-the-scenes praising that would ultimately help the maintenance team win. In turn, the manufacturing team's good relationship with

maintenance helped it become one of the highest pro-
ducers in the plant.

A Model for Group Emotional Intelligence

We've been discussing the need for teams to learn to
channel emotion effectively at the three levels of human
interaction important to them: team to individual member, team to itself, and team to outside entities. Together,
the norms we've been exploring help groups work with
emotions productively and intelligently. Often, groups
with emotionally intelligent members have norms like
these in place, but it's unlikely any group would uncon-
sciously come up with *all* the norms we have outlined. In
other words, this is a model for group emotional intelligence that any work team could benefit from by applying
it deliberately.

What would the ultimate emotionally intelligent team
look like? Closest to the ideal are some of the teams
we've seen at IDEO, the celebrated industrial design firm.
IDEO's creative teams are responsible for the look and
feel of products like Apple's first mouse, the Crest tooth-
paste tube, and the Palm V personal digital assistant.
The firm routinely wins competitions for the form and
function of its designs and even has a business that
teaches creative problem-solving techniques to other
companies.

The nature of IDEO's work calls for high group emotional intelligence. Under pressure of client deadlines
and budget estimates, the company must deliver innovative, aesthetic solutions that balance human needs with
engineering realities. It's a deep philosophical belief at
IDEO that great design is best accomplished through the
creative friction of diverse teams and not the solitary

pursuit of brilliant individuals, so it's imperative that the teams at IDEO click. In our study of those teams, we found group norms supporting emotional intelligence at all three levels of our model.

First, the teams at IDEO are very aware of individual team members' emotions, and they are adept at regulating them. For example, an IDEO designer became very frustrated because someone from marketing was insisting a logo be applied to the designer's product, which he felt would ruin it visually. At a meeting about the product, the team's project leader picked up on the fact that something was wrong. The designer was sitting off by himself, and things "didn't look right." The project leader looked into the situation and then initiated a negotiation that led to a mutual solution.

IDEO team members also confront one another when they break norms. This is common during brainstorming sessions, where the rule is that people must defer judgment and avoid shooting down ideas. If someone breaks that norm, the team comes down on him in a playful yet forceful way (imagine being pelted by foam toys). Or if someone is out of line, the norm is to stand up and call her on it immediately. If a client is in the room, the confrontation is subtler—perhaps a kick under the chair.

Teams at IDEO also demonstrate strengths in group-focused emotional intelligence. To ensure they have a high level of self-awareness, teams constantly seek feedback from both inside and outside the organization. Most important, they work very closely with customers. If a design is not meeting customer expectations, the team finds out quickly and takes steps to modify it.

Regulating group emotion at IDEO often means providing outlets for stress. This is a company that believes in playing and having fun. Several hundred finger blasters (a toy that shoots soft projectiles) have been placed around the building for employees to pick up and start shooting when they're frustrated. Indeed, the design firm's culture welcomes the expression of emotions, so it's not uncommon for someone—whether happy or angry—to stand up and yell. IDEO has even created fun office projects that people can work on if they need a break. For example, they might have a project to design the company holiday card or to design the "tourist stop" displays seen by visitors.

Finally, IDEO teams also have norms to ensure they are aware of the needs and concerns of people outside their boundaries and that they use that awareness to develop relationships with those individuals and groups. On display at IDEO is a curious model: a toy truck with plastic pieces on springs that pop out of the bed of the truck when a button is pressed. It turns out the model commemorates an incident that taught a variety of lessons. The story centers on a design team that had been working for three weeks on a very complex plastic enclosure for a product. Unfortunately, on the Thursday before a Monday client deadline, when an engineer was taking it to be painted, it slipped from his pickup bed and exploded on the road at 70 mph. The team was willing to work through the weekend to rebuild the part but couldn't finish it without the help of the outside fabricator it had used on the original. Because they had taken the time to build a good relationship with the fabricator, its people were willing to go above and beyond the call of duty. The light-hearted display was a way for teammates to show the engineer that all was forgiven— and a reminder to the rest of the organization of how a team in crisis can get by with a little help from its friends.

Where Do Norms Come From?

Not every company is as dependent on teams and their emotional intelligence as IDEO. But now more than ever, we see companies depending on teams for decisions and tasks that, in another time, would have been the work of individuals. And unfortunately, we also see them discovering that a team can have everything going for it—the brightest and most qualified people, access to resources, a clear mission—but still fail because it lacks group emotional intelligence.

Norms that build trust, group identity, and group efficacy are the key to making teams click. They allow an otherwise highly skilled and resourced team to fulfill its potential, and they can help a team faced with substantial challenges achieve surprising victories. So how do norms as powerful as the ones we've described in this article come about? In our research, we saw them being introduced from any of five basic directions: by formal team leaders, by informal team leaders, by courageous followers, through training, or from the larger organizational culture. (For more on how to establish the norms described in this article, see the exhibit "Building Norms for Three Levels of Group Emotional Intelligence.")

At the Hay Group, for example, it was the deliberate action of a team leader that helped one group see the importance of emotions to the group's overall effectiveness. Because this particular group was composed of managers from many different cultures, its leader knew he couldn't assume all the members possessed a high level of interpersonal understanding. To establish that norm, he introduced novelties like having a meeting without a table, using smaller groups, and conducting an inventory of team members' various learning styles.

Building Norms for Three Levels of Group Emotional Intelligence

Group emotional intelligence is about the small acts that make a big difference. It is not about a team member working all night to meet a deadline; it is about saying thank you for doing so. It is not about in-depth discussion of ideas; it is about asking a quiet member for his thoughts. It is not about harmony, lack of tension, and all members liking each other; it is about acknowledging when harmony is false, tension is unexpressed, and treating others with respect. The following exhibit outlines some of the small things that groups can do to establish the norms that build group emotional intelligence.

Individual	Group	Cross-Boundary

NORMS THAT CREATE AWARENESS OF EMOTIONS

Individual	Group	Cross-Boundary
Interpersonal understanding	**Team self-evaluation**	**Organizational understanding**
1. Take time away from group tasks to get to know one another.	1. Schedule time to examine team effectiveness.	1. Find out the concerns and needs of others in the organization.
2. Have a "check in" at the beginning of the meeting—that is, ask how everyone is doing.	2. Create measurable task and process objectives and then measure them.	2. Consider who can influence the team's ability to accomplish its goals.
3. Assume that undesirable behavior takes place for a reason. Find out what that reason is. Ask questions and listen. Avoid negative attributions.	3. Acknowledge and discuss group moods.	3. Discuss the culture and politics in the organization.
4. Tell your teammates what you're thinking and how you're feeling.	4. Communicate your sense of what is transpiring in the team.	4. Ask whether proposed team actions are congruent with the organization's culture and politics.
Perspective taking	5. Allow members to call a "process check." (For instance, a team member might say, "Process check: is this the most effective use of our time right now?")	
1. Ask whether everyone agrees with a decision.		
2. Ask quiet members what they think.	**Seeking feedback**	
3. Question decisions that come too quickly.	1. Ask your "customers" how you are doing.	
4. Appoint a devil's advocate.	2. Post your work and invite comments.	
	3. Benchmark your processes.	

NORMS THAT HELP REGULATE EMOTIONS

Confronting

1. Set ground rules and use them to point out errant behavior.

2. Call members on errant behavior.

3. Create playful devices for pointing out such behavior. These often emerge from the group spontaneously. Reinforce them.

Caring

1. Support members: volunteer to help them if they need it, be flexible, and provide emotional support.

2. Validate members' contributions. Let members know they are valued.

3. Protect members from attack.

4. Respect individuality and differences in perspectives. Listen.

5. Never be derogatory or demeaning.

Creating resources for working with emotion

1. Make time to discuss difficult issues, and address the emotions that surround them.

2. Find creative, shorthand ways to acknowledge and express the emotion in the group.

3. Create fun ways to acknowledge and relieve stress and tension.

4. Express acceptance of members' emotions.

Creating an affirmative environment

1. Reinforce that the team can meet a challenge. Be optimistic. For example, say things like, "We can get through this" or "Nothing will stop us."

2. Focus on what you can control.

3. Remind members of the group's important and positive mission.

4. Remind the group how it solved a similar problem before.

5. Focus on problem solving, not blaming.

Solving problems proactively

1. Anticipate problems and address them before they happen.

2. Take the initiative to understand and get what you need to be effective.

3. Do it yourself if others aren't responding. Rely on yourself, not others.

Building external relationships

1. Create opportunities for networking and interaction.

2. Ask about the needs of other teams.

3. Provide support for other teams.

4. Invite others to team meetings if they might have a stake in what you are doing.

Interventions like these can probably be done only by a formal team leader. The ways informal leaders or other team members enhance emotional intelligence are typically more subtle, though often just as powerful. Anyone might advance the cause, for example, by speaking up if the group appears to be ignoring an important perspective or feeling—or simply by doing his or her part to create an affirmative environment.

Training courses can also go a long way toward increasing emotional awareness and showing people how to regulate emotions. We know of many companies that now focus on emotional issues in leadership development courses, negotiation and communication workshops, and employee-assistance programs like those for stress management. These training programs can sensitize team members to the importance of establishing emotionally intelligent norms.

Finally, perhaps more than anything, a team can be influenced by a broader organizational culture that recognizes and celebrates employee emotion. This is clearly the case at IDEO and, we believe, at many of the companies creating the greatest value in the new economy. Unfortunately, it's the most difficult piece of the puzzle to put in place at companies that don't already have it. For organizations with long histories of employees checking their emotions at the door, change will occur, if at all, one team at a time.

Becoming Intelligent About Emotion

The research presented in this article arose from one simple imperative: in an era of teamwork, it's essential to figure out what makes teams work. Our research shows that, just like individuals, the most effective teams are emotionally intelligent ones—and that any team can attain emotional intelligence.

In this article, we've attempted to lay out a model for positive change, containing the most important types of norms a group can create to enhance its emotional intelligence. Teams, like all groups, operate according to such norms. By working to establish norms for emotional awareness and regulation at all levels of interaction, teams can build the solid foundation of trust, group identity, and group efficacy they need for true cooperation and collaboration—and high performance overall.

Originally published in March 2001
Reprint R0103E

Why Bad Projects Are So Hard to Kill

ISABELLE ROYER

Executive Summary

EVEN AT THE PROTOTYPE STAGE, experts were saying
the technology was obsolete. Yet, in the face of tepid
consumer response, the company stubbornly kept
increasing production capacity and developing new
models. By the time it was finally killed, the initiative had
cost the company an astounding $580 million and had
tied up resources for 14 years.

The product was RCA's SelectaVision videodisc
recorder, and its story is hardly unique. Companies make
similar mistakes—if on a somewhat smaller scale—all the
time.

But why? No one comes to work saying, "I'm going
to pursue a project that will waste my company millions
of dollars." Quite the opposite. They come to work full of
excitement about a project they believe in. And that, surprisingly, can be the root of all the trouble—a fervent

53

belief in the inevitability of a project's ultimate success. Starting, naturally enough, with a project's champion, this faith can spread throughout the organization, leading everyone to believe collectively in the product's viability and to view any signs of impending doom merely as temporary setbacks.

This phenomenon is documented here in two chillingly detailed case studies, one involving Essilor, the world's largest maker of corrective lenses for eyeglasses, and the other involving Lafarge, the largest producer of building materials. By counterexample, they point the way toward avoiding such morasses: assembling project teams not entirely composed of like-minded people and putting in place—and sticking to—well-defined review processes. Both cases also show that if it takes a project champion to get a project up and running, it may take a new kind of organizational player—an "exit champion"— to push an irrationally exuberant organization to admit when enough is enough.

Y OU CAN STILL FIND THEM on eBay, sleek and gleaming videodisc players with LP-sized discs. The product: RCA's SelectaVision—one of the biggest consumer electronics flops of all time.

But it isn't simply the monumental failure in the marketplace that makes the SelectaVision story worth remembering. It's that RCA insisted on plowing money into the product long after all signs pointed to near certain failure. When the company developed its first prototype in 1970, some experts already considered the phonograph-like technology obsolete. Seven years later, with the quality of VCRs improving and digital technology on the horizon, every one of RCA's competitors had abandoned videodisc research. Even in the face of tepid consumer response to SelectaVision's launch in 1981, RCA continued to develop new models and invest in production capacity. When the product was finally killed in 1984, it had cost the company an astounding $580 million and had tied up resources for 14 years.

Companies make similar mistakes—if on a somewhat more modest scale—all the time. Of course, hindsight is 20/20; it's easy after the fact to criticize bold bets that didn't pay off. But too often managers charge ahead in the face of mounting evidence that success is pretty well unachievable.

Why can't companies kill projects that are clearly doomed? Is it just poor management? Bureaucratic inertia? My research has uncovered something quite different. Hardly the product of managerial incompetence or entrenched bureaucracy, the failures I've examined resulted, ironically, from a fervent and widespread belief among managers in the inevitability of their projects' ultimate success. This sentiment typically originates, naturally enough, with a project's champion; it then spreads throughout the organization, often to the highest levels, reinforcing itself each step of the way. The result is what I call collective belief, and it can lead an otherwise rational organization into some very irrational behavior.

Of course, a strongly held conviction and the refusal to let inevitable setbacks undermine it are just what you need to get a project up and running. But there is a dark side: As the project moves forward, faith can blind you to increasingly negative feedback—from the lab, from vendors and partners, from customers.

To better understand why this happens and what can be done to prevent it, I analyzed two failed product innovations at two large French companies. (For a brief description of my research, see "What Were They Thinking?" at the end of this article.) One was a new lens created by Essilor, the world's largest maker of corrective lenses for eyeglasses. The other was an industrial additive used in manufacturing paper, paint, and plastics, developed by Lafarge, the largest producer of building materials. In both cases, the projects absorbed millions of dollars of investment before the companies finally abandoned them.

My analysis revealed a number of practices that can help companies avoid this kind of disaster. For one, they can assemble project teams not entirely composed of people enthusiastically singing from the same hymnbook. They can put in place a well-defined review process—and then follow it. Perhaps most important, companies need to recognize the role of "exit champions": managers with the temperament and credibility to question the prevailing belief, demand hard data on the viability of the project, and, if necessary, forcefully make the case that it should be killed. While the importance of project champions is well documented, the value of someone who is able to pull the plug on a project before it becomes a money sink hasn't generally been appreciated.

Faith That Wouldn't Be Shattered

Essilor has long been proud of its research. In 1959, it invented the Varilux "progressive" lens, for instance, which corrects both near- and farsightedness without the telltale lines that denote traditional bifocals. But this story starts in the summer of 1979, when a similar breakthrough appears possible. Since 1974, the company has been working on a composite glass-and-plastic material that's lightweight, shatter resistant, scratch resistant, and light sensitive. Now a researcher has come up with a way to make a lens from this material. Essilor's research manager immediately takes a personal interest in the idea, and he orders the creation of a trial lens. Two days later, it's done.

The news spreads quickly throughout the company and is greeted enthusiastically. The research manager seeks and gets approval to proceed with additional research. The CEO himself helps select the managers who will oversee the project, many of whom have worked together on the Varilux lens and other successful projects.

Early on, some questions are raised about the potential cost of this new composite lens, as well as its durability. It's common for layers of any composite material to separate. Indeed, the director of research and manufacturing questions whether the product is even viable. But his concern isn't heeded because he is, as one colleague says, "always skeptical." No initial marketing studies are conducted, but none had been done for Varilux, either; in both cases, the projects are driven by the exciting technology. Based on the current sales of other Essilor products, internal estimates predict sales of nearly 40 million units a year by 1985. In April 1980, the project is accepted for development and a target launch date is set for late 1981. Excitement is high.

In September 1980 though, some bad news arrives: Corning, which supplies the glass for the composite lens, says that meeting the U.S. Food and Drug Administration's test for shatter resistance is proving more difficult than expected. If this continues to be the case, company estimates indicate that sales in 1985 will total just 10 million units. Then, pilot tests in January 1981 reveal a number of other problems, including a tendency of the lens to crack as it's mounted into the frame. Researchers are confident that this problem can be solved (though the company later decides it will offer an exchange guarantee to opticians). Despite the problems revealed in the pilot test, production facilities are built, and trial manufacturing begins. But now another issue arises: Production costs turn out to be twice what was forecast, which will make the lens as much as six times as expensive as normal lenses.

Essilor proudly launches the lens in June 1982. The president of the company sends a sample to the French Ministry of Industry. One researcher tucks a prototype away in his attic so that he can someday show his son "how you do innovation." The manager who unveils the lens at a press conference says he feels a sense of "real jubilation."

Customers are less enthusiastic: Opticians complain about the price and the difficulties of mounting the lens. Essilor has forecast sales of 200,000 units by the end of 1982, a number limited solely by initial production capacity. But sales reach just 20,000 by that date. What's more, concerns about the tendency of the lens's layers to separate are proving justified.

These setbacks are an emotional blow to those involved in the project but are not enough to destroy their belief. "It felt like a knockout," one recalls. "Still, although we were in shock, we knew failure was impossible." After all, those involved point out, initial sales of Varilux had also been slow, because people found the progressive lens difficult to get used to.

The problems continue. In 1985, Essilor launches a second-generation lens meant to fix the separation problems, but it fails to do so. Sales drop below 15,000 units a year. In 1986, a modified composite material solves the separation problem, but the lens remains difficult for opticians to mount in the frame. Researchers are asked to fix this problem before the company will commit itself to launching a third-generation lens.

After a year of further research, the problem still isn't solved. But the research manager argues to the executive committee that, since the separation problem has been corrected, the third-generation lens should be launched. The company does so at the end of 1987, and, in 1988, sales grow to a lackluster 50,000 units.

Then, in the spring of 1989, because of retirements and a restructuring of the company's overall research and production activities, four new managers join the project. A new research manager replaces the lens's foremost champion. In September, the new research manager completes his own evaluation of the project. Sales are still low, and the U.S. market remains out of reach because the lens still hasn't passed the FDA test. The investment needed to develop a full range of products, including a progressive lens, could double what has been spent so far. He recommends that the lens be abandoned.

Top management rejects his recommendation. The company does decide, however, to conduct a thorough evaluation of the project. To no one's surprise, a business analysis shows that the lens currently doesn't generate a profit. But a marketing study further concludes that even if the quality problems are ironed out, potential sales will reach only 1.5 million units per year, a fraction of the 40 million originally predicted. The implication: The lens will never be very profitable.

In September 1990, with quality problems still unsolved and no prospect of passing the FDA test, the company decides to call an immediate halt to research on the lens and stop production within a year. It's been ten years since the first warning signs arose. It has cost Essilor Fr 300 million, or more than $50 million in 1990 dollars.

A Belief in Crystals

Lafarge, like Essilor, has a big stake in the success of the product it is developing. It's early 1985, and research that Lafarge has done on the crystallization of gypsum, a mineral commonly used in the company's core building-materials businesses, looks like it is about to bear fruit. The engineering manager of the gypsum division has concluded that the crystals could serve as a superior substitute for the ground-up minerals commonly used in making paper and paint. The market could be large: One internal forecast puts potential annual sales at Fr 400 million, or about $40 million at the time. And pride as well as profit is at stake. Lafarge has typically grown through acquisition; here is a chance for the company to prove it can grow organically by leveraging its resources into new businesses.

Later that year, the engineering manager of the gypsum division begins research on the use of the crystals as a paper filler (something added to paper stock to improve such physical or optical properties as texture or opacity). He finds a partner in a big paper producer, Aussedat Rey. The engineering manager and his boss, the division's director of operations, seek and receive project backing from Lafarge's top management. Because the crystal-based approach is so innovative, enthusiasm quickly grows.

Over the next several years, the project enjoys both successes and setbacks. The paper filler product is superior in a number of ways to existing fillers, and the crystals turn out to have another potential application in plastics manufacturing. Aussedat Rey agrees to pay for further paper filler tests.

These highlight several problems. The product has the potential to clog certain papermaking machines. And it is not concentrated enough, making it relatively expensive for customers to use. Researchers are confident, however, that these problems can be solved. Lafarge's top management accepts the project for development, including applications for paper, paint, and plastics, and sets 1990 as the target launch date.

Aussedat Rey's first production trial of the paper filler in December 1987 is a technical success, although the paper company still wants a more concentrated version. The successful trial heightens Lafarge's optimism; informal estimates of annual sales grow to Fr 1 billion, or about $190 million in 1988 dollars. To be sure, projections indicate that the paper filler itself probably won't be profitable. But the full range of products for paper, paint, and plastics taken together should be. Unfortunately, only the paper filler has advanced beyond the laboratory stage.

Still, people are eager to get the product to market. To begin production in 1990, the gypsum division's director of operations needs funding to break ground on the plant in 1989. At the end of 1988, Lafarge's top management, aware that tests on the more-concentrated version of the paper filler have not yet been run, approves funding for the plant, so long as certain criteria are met. Before the money is released, the project team must have "verified the feasibility of the manufacturing process in the pilot workshop and the product's quality and acceptability to customers."

This tentative go-ahead is greeted enthusiastically by project members. A lone dissenting voice is Lafarge's new mineral-fillers manager, recently recruited from a consumer products company. He raises concerns about remaining technical challenges, especially after a more-concentrated version of the paper filler fails a new test at Aussedat Rey. But his concerns are generally ignored because of his lack of experience in industrial products. In fact, others involved in the project repeatedly remind him of this fact. He stops raising questions—and ultimately resigns.

Meanwhile, Aussedat Rey is showing less interest in the paper filler and repeatedly delays further trials. (It later will sever its relationship with Lafarge because the price of the paper filler is too high.) The paper filler's "quality and acceptability to customers"—the criteria that must be met to receive funding for the plant—seem far from assured. And yet, after a presentation by members of the project, top management gives the plant a green light, and it is inaugurated in September 1990. Several weeks later, at Lafarge's annual meeting of researchers from labs across the company, the paper filler researchers and their managers present the project as an example of a successful internal research initiative.

But the new plant remains idle, as no product has yet emerged from the lab that is ready for production and no customer or partner has been found to fund further tests.

Meanwhile, one of the project's champions, the gypsum division's director of operations, has left Lafarge for health reasons and has been replaced by an operations director from another division of the company. He forms a task force to formally evaluate the viability of the project. This isn't easy because of the lack of data. For example, although an initial market study was done, there have been no follow-ups to gauge demand for a product that is now likely to lack some of the features originally envisioned. Still, in April 1991, the task force's report confirms that the paper filler itself won't be profitable and estimates that two years and another Fr 30 million (about $5.3 million in 1991 dollars) would be needed to get other products ready for pilot testing. The new director of operations recommends terminating the project.

Most team members agree with the factual findings, but many reject the recommendation that the project be killed. So, although top management stops development of the paper filler, it authorizes continued research on products to be used in paper coating and plastics manufacturing. At the end of 1991, however, a test of the paper-coating product produces poor results and offers little hope that it can be improved. In early 1992, the plant is sold and the entire project is stopped, having cost a total of Fr 150 million (nearly $30 million in 1992 dollars) over seven years.

The Seductive Appeal of Collective Belief

So what got into the decision makers at these two companies? Why did Essilor persist with the development of its new lens in the face of so much negative evidence? Why did Lafarge build a brand-new production facility before determining whether its gypsum crystal additive had a future in the marketplace?

These were not cases of bureaucratic inertia. If anything, the procedures and controls over these projects were too lax rather than too unresponsive or inflexible. Nor were these cases in which project champions were flogging a dead horse to justify their original touting of it. What the many interviews and myriad contemporary documents reveal in both companies is the power, and troublesome implications, of a very human impulse: the desire to believe in something—in these situations, in the projects' ultimate success. In both companies, this belief was held not just by a handful of individuals but by much of their organizations.

How does that happen? Collective belief arises because individual belief is often contagious, particularly when it reinforces others' perceptions and desires. When this is the case, the belief can spread easily among the various decision makers who control a project's fate. Here's how that played out at Lafarge and Essilor.

THE EMERGENCE OF BELIEF

The original true believer is a project champion, who holds an unyielding conviction—based, often as not, on a hunch rather than on strong evidence—that a project will succeed. This belief then spreads to others; how quickly and with what intensity depends on a number of factors. Some of these are organizational and some are particular to the champion—for example, his personal credibility and charisma and the robustness and range of his social network within the company. Indeed, if the champion's reputation is strong enough, the belief can pass from person to person until it is shared by individuals who don't even know the champion and know little of the project. At Lafarge, two project members candidly admitted that they couldn't truly assess the potential of the new product but took the word of one of the project's champions that it was a winner.

Belief in a project is all the more contagious when its ultimate success is something that people greatly desire.

For both Essilor and Lafarge, the two projects furthered important companywide goals: the development of products that embodied a strong technological tradition of "research for the sake of vision" at Essilor, and the desire to generate organic growth rather than growth through acquisition at Lafarge.

But a project can also satisfy individual desires, ones that are often quite various and even potentially conflicting. Some at Essilor reported they saw the lens as something "that would permanently eliminate competitors." Others hoped the project would maintain employment levels in the glass factories as plastic lenses grew in popularity. Some senior executives saw the composite glass-and-plastic lens as a way to strengthen corporate culture: Essilor was born from the merger of Essel, a glass-lens manufacturer, and Silor, a rival that made plastic lenses, and the two divisions still competed against each other.

At Lafarge, some viewed the new additive as a way to enhance the reputation of the company's R&D function. Others saw it as a strategically important move beyond building materials. In both companies, the collective belief served as an umbrella that sheltered an array of hopes and dreams; those, in turn, worked together to reinforce the collective belief.

THE PERSISTENCE OF BELIEF

Once a collective belief takes hold, it tends to perpetuate itself. For one thing, groups have a way of drowning out dissent. At Essilor and Lafarge, both lone initial dissidents—Essilor's director of research and manufacturing and Lafarge's mineral-fillers manager—were generally ignored or told that the questions they raised reflected their lack of experience or competence. Eventually, they stopped raising questions. This self-censorship gave the groups an illusion of unanimity and invulnerability, which in turn helped sustain individual belief. One manager at Essilor said that the lens's failure in the market in 1982 raised doubts in his mind. But he chose not to voice these and, because of the group's apparent unanimity, soon forgot them.

Curiously, setbacks, rather than undermining faith, often drive people to work all the harder to maintain it. Despite the Essilor lens's poor market performance, the company continued to produce it in vast quantities, consistently more than were sold. Since project members believed the market failure was only a prelude to ultimate success, they exhibited what one manager called "technological relentlessness" in their pursuit of both improvements and customers.

This intensity is not surprising, given the emotional attachment people feel for a project they passionately believe in. As one Essilor manager said of an early version of the lens: "It was a dream, and a dream come true on top of that! The product existed! It was beautiful." Another manager, recalling a setback in lens development, observed, "We didn't dare wonder whether we should stop or not. It was too hard."

THE CONSEQUENCES OF BELIEF

The greatest danger posed by an organization's collective belief in a project is that problems, even if acknowledged, won't be seen as signs of failure—or at least as issues that should be resolved before moving on to the next stage of development. At Essilor, some managers explained away the lukewarm initial demand for the lens as an aberration related to the soon-to-be-solved technical problem of layer separation, forgetting that the market was generally unaware of this problem. At Lafarge, one manager knew that the decision to build the plant was probably premature, given the available test results for the product, but he said nothing because he was eager to move forward on an enterprise everyone was certain would succeed. Managers at both companies referred to the blindness that resulted from their faith in the projects.

This blindness persists in part because collective belief undermines normal organizational procedures and safeguards. For one thing, the enthusiasm generated by faith in a project can lead to an unrealistically tight development timetable. Essilor canceled some tests and substituted shorter, less reliable ones in order to stick to its aggressive development schedule. A test to see how durable the lenses remained over time, for example, was shortened from two years to six months. Lafarge's desire to remain on schedule was the driving force in the construction of the plant before necessary tests on the additive had been completed.

Enthusiasm also can result in lenient procedures for reviewing the viability of a product throughout its development. For instance, scratch-resistance specifications for Essilor's new lens were not defined until 1990, eight years after the product was initially launched. Furthermore, widespread enthusiasm can lead to the formation of a project team filled with, and overseen by, uncritical boosters of the initiative.

Together, these factors can create a reinforcing chain that perpetuates collective belief. Decision makers' faith in the project results in an absence of clear decision criteria, which leads to ambiguous information, which in turn favors wishful thinking by those decision makers and further bolsters their belief in the project's success. In a sense, the project takes on a life of its own.

Avoiding the Dangers of Blind Faith

In your own company, you have undoubtedly known projects that dragged on but went nowhere. You may be aware of a handful of bad projects that are grinding along, or even picking up speed, right now. How can companies prevent this sort of thing? How could the managers at Essilor, for example, have known that the composite lens project wouldn't turn out the way the Varilux lens effort did?

They probably couldn't, at least for a while. But they could have done a number of things that would have made them better able to judge their progress and counteract the distorting effects of collective belief. Two kinds of safeguards can be built into a project before it even gets under way. Another one requires a manager involved in a project to play an important, new role.

BEWARE OF CHEERLEADING SQUADS

All too often, project teams are self-selected. They include people who have volunteered because they share an initial enthusiasm for the project. They may even have worked together on successful projects in the past. They know the drill and can anticipate one another's moves. In fact, they know them too well. As they interact, there are none of the awkward missteps or misunderstandings that can produce unexpected insights—or signs of trouble. Warning flags that do appear may be ignored; after all, everyone is rooting for something they believe in.

Executives launching a project would do well, then, to include skeptics along with believers in the project teams from the outset, paying particular attention to those who will be directly involved in making decisions. Then, over the course of the initiative, some decision makers should be replaced with others, who will look at the project with fresh eyes.

At Essilor and Lafarge, top management populated the projects with true believers. In fact, in both cases, the sole initial critics joined the projects somewhat by chance. Essilor's director of research and manufacturing was involved only because he was the immediate supervisor of the manager of the plant where the lens would be made. Lafarge's mineral-fillers manager had originally been hired for another job and joined the project only because Lafarge had difficulty finding someone with both minerals and project expertise to fill out the team. At Essilor, personal relationships also came into play; some members had been friends for 20 years—a further reason that robust criticism, which might jeopardize those friendships, didn't emerge.

Only when turnover occurred for reasons unrelated to the project—retirement, health problems, the restructuring of a companywide research function—was the cohesiveness of the project groups disrupted and some measure of objectivity introduced.

ESTABLISH AN EARLY WARNING SYSTEM

From the start, no matter how exciting or important a project is, a company needs to make sure that its control procedures and criteria for evaluating project viability at each stage of development are truly working—that they are clearly defined, rigorous, and actually met. Big companies like Essilor and Lafarge typically have these kinds of effective internal controls for all sorts of processes— for example, "stage gates" that companies must go through as they proceed with a potential acquisition. But they can easily forget to establish such structures at the beginning of a project that seems bound for glory. Or even if they do establish processes for good decision making, they can end up ignoring them—or the results— amid the excitement generated by a new project.

Lafarge executives concede that they failed to adhere to their own decision criteria when they went ahead and built the plant—although the criteria were vague enough to make this fairly easy to do. Essilor had several clear procedures for testing the lens during development that weren't followed; others produced negative results, which were ignored. As one Essilor manager said: "The decision to launch was implicit. It was just a question of when."

RECOGNIZE THE ROLE OF THE EXIT CHAMPION

Sometimes it takes an individual, rather than growing evidence, to shake the collective belief of a project team. If the problem with unbridled enthusiasm starts as an unintended consequence of the legitimate work of a project champion, then what may be needed is a countervailing force—an exit champion. These people are more than devil's advocates. Instead of simply raising questions about a project, they seek objective evidence showing that problems in fact exist. This allows them to challenge—or, given the ambiguity of existing data, conceivably even to confirm—the viability of a project. They then take action based on the data. At both Essilor and Lafarge, exit champions—the new research manager at Essilor, and the new operations director at Lafarge—joined the projects as evidence of their unpromising futures was mounting. But supporters were still clinging to the shreds of positive evidence that occasionally emerged—or ignoring the evidence altogether. Had it not been for these exit champions, team members said later, the projects probably would have continued for months or even years.

To be effective, an exit champion needs to be directly involved in the project; a negative assessment from someone based elsewhere in the company is too easy to dismiss as ill-informed or motivated by organizational rivalry. The exit champion also needs a high degree of personal credibility. The managers at Essilor and Lafarge who had raised questions about the lens and paper filler during the early development stages lacked this credibility. Essilor's director of research and manufacturing was known within the organization as a naysayer; Lafarge's mineral-fillers manager, who came from another company, appeared to lack industry experience. The exit champions, by contrast, had been with their companies for a long time and were well regarded by top management. Both had a strong network of people at different levels of the company ready to provide support when they decided the project should be killed.

What kind of person would willingly assume such a role? Even if killing a project doesn't put an exit champion out of a job—the individuals at Essilor and Lafarge had responsibilities beyond the projects in question—the role, unlike that of a traditional project champion, seems to offer little in the way of prestige or other personal rewards. (For a discussion of the differences between the two roles, see "The Exit Champion and the Project Champion" at the end of this article.) In fact, the exit champion faces inevitable hostility from project supporters; those at Essilor and Lafarge were variously described as villains or dream breakers.

Consequently, exit champions need to be fearless, willing to put their reputations on the line and face the likelihood of exclusion from the camaraderie of the project team. They need to be determined: Both Essilor's and Lafarge's exit champions failed in their first attempts to stop their projects. Perhaps most important, exit champions need to have some incentive for putting themselves out to halt a bad project. For many, this will simply be an acute distaste for wasted effort. As one exit champion at another company I researched said, "When I work, I need to believe in what I do. I don't want to waste time on something that is worthless."

It is important to understand that an exit champion is not a henchman sent by top management to kill the project. The exit champions at Essilor and Lafarge certainly weren't: They were assigned their positions only because their predecessors had left the company, and they simply took the initiative to determine if their projects were likely to be successful. Indeed, it wasn't initially clear to either of them that their respective projects *should* be killed. Although signs that the projects wouldn't succeed were accumulating, in neither case was the evidence conclusive because it wasn't based on hard data.

Senior executives need to recognize the exit champion as a defined role that someone might play in the organization—otherwise, they may not know an exit champion for who he is and give him the support he will need. And they can take steps to create an environment in which such a savior would be more likely to emerge. Just as companies celebrate and recount stories of the great successes of product champions, they could perhaps identify and spread tales of courageous exit champions in their midst (or at other companies) who saved their organizations millions of dollars. Top managers should at the least make it clear that challenges to a popular project would be welcome or even rewarded. At the same time, though, they need to demand from the exit champion strong evidence of the project's weaknesses— just as they should have earlier demanded growing evidence of its viability.

It Couldn't Happen Here

When all is said and done, do Essilor's and Lafarge's experiences—not to mention RCA's in the case of its ill-fated SelectaVision—simply reflect bad business judgment? Were they nothing more nor less than dumb business moves? Aren't situations like these unlikely to be repeated at your company?

Don't bet on it. Although they may not always be played out on such a grand scale, stories like these are all too familiar in business. That's because belief is a powerful sentiment, and collective belief is even more powerful. Clearly, any project has to start with faith because there typically isn't much objective evidence, if any, at the beginning to justify it. But, as a project unfolds and investments increase, this faith has to be increasingly tested against the data. Indeed, the challenge for managers in the "can-do" culture of business is to distinguish between belief as a key driver of success—and belief as something that can blind managers to a project's ultimate failure.

What Were They Thinking?

HOW DO YOU GET AN accurate picture of an organization's belief in a project, especially after the fact? My study of Essilor and Lafarge, which was conducted several years after the two projects analyzed in this article were abandoned, lasted two years. It included several dozen interviews with middle managers and senior executives involved in the projects. I also had access to a range of company documents: reports, memos, written notes, test results, marketing studies, business plans, and, in each case, the analysis of an outside consultant. Finally, for each company, I asked two executives—each with a different view of the project—to review the lengthy written summary of the project history I had prepared.

Researching events long after the fact can provide perspective that would be absent from contemporary research. But there is the danger that people's perceptions and conclusions will be colored because the project's outcome is known. To guard against this, all technical evaluations came from documents written during the course of the project. In interviews, I asked people what their opinions and feelings were at the time, not what they thought now. Later, I cross-checked the interview data with the written record. When there was a conflict, I went back to the interviewees to ask for more details until the data were consistent.

The Exit Champion and the Project Champion

AT BOTH ESSILOR AND LAFARGE, some of the projects' champions opposed the exit champions who successfully pulled the plugs on their projects. Although no public confrontations occurred in either case, the project champions raised with other project participants questions about the exit champions' intentions.

Such conflicts are interesting because in many ways the roles of the traditional project champion and the exit champion are similar. Just as innovations are unlikely to be implemented without champions, failing projects are unlikely to be halted without exit champions. In fact, the types of individuals who gravitate toward those roles are also similar.

Both project champions and exit champions must show initiative; after all, they have by definition assumed their roles rather than been assigned them. And they need to be energetic and determined enough to overcome the obstacles and inevitable skepticism they face. Given their similar personal traits, it's not surprising that, at a number of companies I studied, exit champions had been project champions at other points in their careers.

Differences between project champions and exit champions appear, however, in the particulars. For one thing, while project champions necessarily operate in an environment of uncertainty and ambiguity, exit champions need to remove ambiguity. They must gather hard data that will be convincing enough to overcome the opposition of believers. They need clear criteria for deciding whether to kill the project. When existing procedures don't include such criteria, they need to reach an agreement with believers on the criteria for assessing the new data; otherwise, reaching an agreement on the decision will be impossible. Thus, while project champions often violate procedures, exit champions typically have to introduce or restore them.

Project champions' reputations are often put at risk by their choice to champion what may turn out to be a failed project. Exit champions also put their reputations at risk, but the threat is of a different nature. Project champions run a long-term risk of being wrong—something that will become clear only if a project ultimately fails. Exit champions face the immediate risk that comes from challenging a popular project. That risk exists even if the exit champion is, in fact, ultimately right.

Originally published in February 2003
Reprint R0302C

Speeding Up Team Learning

AMY EDMONDSON, RICHARD BOHMER, AND
GARY PISANO

Executive Summary

CARDIAC SURGERY IS ONE OF medicine's modern miracles. In an operating room no larger than many household kitchens, a patient is rendered functionally dead while a surgical team repairs or replaces damaged arteries or valves. Each operation requires incredible teamwork—a single error can have disastrous consequences. In other words, surgical teams are not all that different from the cross-functional teams that have become crucial to business success.

The challenge of team management these days is not simply to execute existing processes efficiently. It's to implement new processes—as quickly as possible. But adopting new technologies or new business processes is highly disruptive, regardless of industry. The authors studied how surgical teams at 16 major medical centers implemented a difficult new procedure for performing

77

cardiac surgery. The setting was ideal for rigorously focusing on how teams learn and why some learn faster than others.

The authors found that the most successful teams had leaders who actively managed the groups' learning efforts. Teams that most successfully implemented the new technology shared three essential characteristics. They were designed for learning; their leader framed the challenge so that team members were highly motivated to learn; and an environment of psychological safety fostered communication and innovation.

The finding that teams learn more quickly if they are explicitly managed for learning poses a challenge in many areas of business. Team leaders in business tend to be chosen more for their technical expertise than for their management skills. Team leaders need to become adept at creating learning environments, and senior managers need to look beyond technical competence and identify leaders who can motivate and manage teams of disparate specialists.

CARDIAC SURGERY IS ONE OF medicine's modern miracles. In an operating room no larger than many household kitchens, a patient is rendered functionally dead—the heart no longer beating, the lungs no longer breathing—while a surgical team repairs or replaces damaged arteries or valves. A week later, the patient walks out of the hospital.

The miracle is a testament to medical technology— but also to incredible teamwork. A cardiac surgical team includes an array of specialists who need to work in close cooperation for the operation to succeed. A single error, miscommunication, or slow response can have disastrous consequences. In other words, surgical teams are not all that different from the cross-functional teams that in recent years have become crucial to business success.

We studied how surgical teams at 16 major medical centers implemented a difficult new procedure for performing cardiac surgery. What we found sheds light on one of the key determinants of team performance: a team's ability to adapt to a new way of working. In corporate settings, teams frequently have to learn new technologies or processes that are designed to improve performance. Often, however, things get worse—sometimes for a long time—before they get better. Team members may find it hard to break out of deeply ingrained routines. Or they may struggle to adjust to new roles and communication requirements.

When a product development team adopts computer-aided design tools, for example, designers, test engineers, process engineers, and even marketers have to learn the technology. But they also have to create and become comfortable with entirely new relationships, working collaboratively instead of making contributions individually and then handing pieces of the project off to the next person.

Most teams become proficient at new tasks or processes over time. But time is a luxury few teams—or companies—have. If you move too slowly, you may find that competitors are reaping the benefits of a new technology while you're still in the learning stages or that an even newer technology has superseded the one you're finally integrating into your work. The challenge of team management these days is not simply to execute existing processes efficiently. It's to implement new processes—as quickly as possible.

Whether in a hospital or an office park, getting a team up to speed isn't easy. As a surgeon on one of the teams we studied wryly put it, the new surgical procedure represented "a transfer of pain—from the patient to the surgeon." But if that came as no surprise, we *were* surprised at some of the things that helped, or didn't help, certain teams learn faster than others. An overriding lesson was that the most successful teams had leaders who actively managed their teams' learning efforts. That finding is likely to pose a challenge in many areas of business where, as in medicine, team leaders are chosen more for their technical expertise than for their management skills.

Teamwork in Operation

A conventional cardiac operation, which typically lasts two to four hours, unites four professions and a battery of specialized equipment in a carefully choreographed routine. The surgeon and the surgeon's assistant are supported by a scrub nurse, a cardiac anesthesiologist, and a perfusionist—a technician who runs the bypass machine that takes over the functions of the heart and lungs. A team in a typical cardiac surgery department performs hundreds of open-heart operations a year. Consequently, the well-defined sequence of individual tasks that constitute an operation becomes so routine that team members often don't need words to signal the start of a new stage in the procedure; a mere look is enough.

Open-heart surgery has saved countless lives, but its invasiveness—the surgeon must cut open the patient's chest and split the breastbone—has meant a painful and lengthy recovery. Recently, however, a new technology has enabled surgical teams to perform "minimally invasive cardiac surgery" in which the surgeon works through a relatively small incision between the ribs. The procedure, introduced in hospitals in the late 1990s, held out the promise of a much shorter and more pleasant recovery for thousands of patients—and a potential competitive advantage for the hospitals that adopted it. (For a description of the procedure, see "A New Way to Mend a Broken Heart" at the end of this article.)

Although the scene and players remain the same, the new technology significantly alters the nature of the surgical team's work. Obviously, individual team members need to learn new tasks. The surgeon, with the heart no longer laid out in full view, has to operate without the visual and tactile cues that typically guide this painstaking work. The anesthesiologist has to use ultrasound imaging equipment, never before a part of cardiac operations. But the mastery of new tasks isn't the only challenge. In the new procedure, a number of familiar tasks occur in a different sequence, requiring a team to unlearn the old routine before learning the new one.

More subtly, the new technology requires greater interdependence and communication among team members. For example, much of the information about the patient's heart that the surgeon traditionally gleaned through sight and touch is now delivered via digital readouts and ultrasound images displayed on monitors out of his or her field of vision. Thus the surgeon must rely on team members for essential information, disrupting not only the team's routine but also the surgeon's role as order giver in the operating room's tightly structured hierarchy.

Isolating the "Fast Factors"

The 16 teams we studied were among those that adopted this demanding new procedure. Given its complexity, they exercised great care in carrying it out, checking and double-checking every step. As a result, the rate of deaths and serious complications was no higher than for conventional procedures. But the teams were taking too long. At every hospital we studied, operations using the new technology initially took two to three times longer than conventional open-heart procedures.

Time is important in cardiac surgery. Long operations put patients at risk and strain operating teams, both mentally and physically. And with operating-room time costly and profit margins for cardiac surgery relatively high, cash-strapped hospitals want to maximize the number of operations cardiac teams perform daily.

As teams at the various hospitals struggled with the new procedure, they did get faster. This underscored one of the key tenets of learning, that the more you do something, the better you get at it. But a striking fact emerged from our research: The pace of improvement differed dramatically from team to team. Our goal was to find out what allowed certain teams to extract disproportionate amounts of learning from each increment of experience and thereby learn more quickly than their counterparts at other hospitals.

The adoption of the new technology provided an ideal laboratory for rigorously studying how teams learn and why some learn faster than others. We collected detailed data on 660 patients who underwent minimally invasive cardiac surgery at the 16 medical centers, beginning with each team's first such operation. We also interviewed in person all staff members who were involved in adopting the technology. Then we used standard statistical methods to analyze how quickly procedure times fell with accumulated experience, adjusting for variables that might influence operating time, such as the type of operation and the patient's condition. Using these and other data, we also assessed the technology implementation effort at each hospital.

Because teams doing conventional cardiac surgery follow widely accepted protocols and use standardized technology, the teams adopting the new procedure started with a common set of practices and norms. They also received the same three-day training program in the new technology. This consistency among teams in both their traditional work practices and their preparation for the new task helped us zero in on the "fast factors" that allowed some teams to adopt the technology relatively quickly.

Rethinking Conventional Wisdom

We were surprised by some of the factors that turned out not to matter in how quickly teams learned. For instance, variations among the teams in educational background and surgical experience didn't necessarily have any impact on the steepness of the learning curve. (For a comparison of teams at two medical centers, see "A Tale of Two Hospitals" at the end of this article.)

We also turned up evidence that countered several cherished notions about the ways organizations—and, by implication, teams—adopt new technologies and processes. For one thing, high-level management support for the minimally invasive technology wasn't decisive in hospitals' success in implementing it. At some hospitals, implementation was unsuccessful despite strong vocal and financial support from senior officials. At others, teams enjoyed tremendous success despite support that was ambivalent at best. For example, one surgeon initially had difficulty convincing hospital administrators that the new procedure should be tried there; they saw it as a time-consuming distraction that might benefit surgeons but would further tax the overworked hospital staff. Even so, the surgeon's team became one of the more successful in our study.

The status of the surgeon who led the team also didn't seem to make a difference. Conventional wisdom holds that a team charged with implementing a new technology or process needs a leader who has clout within the organization—someone who can "make things happen" in support of the team's efforts. But we saw situations in which department heads and world-renowned cardiac surgeons couldn't get their teams to adapt to the new operating routine. At other sites, relatively junior surgeons championed the new technology and, with little support from more senior colleagues, brought their teams quickly along the learning curve.

Finally, the debriefs, project audits, and after-action reports so often cited as key to learning weren't pivotal to the success or failure of the teams we studied. In fact, few surgical teams had time for regular, formal reviews of their work. At one hospital, such reviews were normally conducted at midnight over take-out Chinese food. Some research-oriented academic medical centers did aggregate performance data and analyze the data retrospectively, but teams at these hospitals didn't necessarily improve at faster rates. Instead, as we will discuss, the successful teams engaged in real-time learning—analyzing and drawing lessons from the process while it was under way.

Creating a Learning Team

We found that success in learning came down to the way teams were put together and how they drew on their experiences—in other words, on the teams' design and management. Teams that learned the new procedure most quickly shared three essential characteristics. They were designed for learning; their leaders framed the challenge in such a way that team members were highly motivated to learn; and the leaders' behavior created an environment of psychological safety that fostered communication and innovation.

DESIGNING A TEAM FOR LEARNING

Team leaders often have considerable discretion in determining, through choice of members, the group's mix of skills and areas of expertise. The teams in our study had no such leeway—cardiac surgery requires a surgeon, an anesthesiologist, a perfusionist, and a scrub nurse. But the leaders who capitalized on the opportunity to choose particular individuals from those specialties reaped significant benefits.

At one extreme, the leaders—the surgeons—took little initiative in choosing team members. At one hospital, the staff members chosen for training in the procedure were, essentially, those who happened to be available the weekend of the training session.

In a few teams, however, selection was much more collaborative, and the choices were carefully weighed. An anesthesiology department head, for instance, might get significant input from the cardiac surgeon before choosing an anesthesiologist. Selection was based not only on competence but also on such factors as the individual's ability to work with others, willingness to deal with new and ambiguous situations, and confidence in offering suggestions to team members with higher status.

Another critical aspect of team design was the degree to which substitutions were permitted. In conventional surgery, all members of the surgical department are assumed to be equally capable of doing the work of their particular discipline, and team members within a discipline are readily substituted for one another. It's logical to assume that training additional team members would allow for more cases to be performed using the new procedure, but we found that such flexibility has a cost. Reductions in average procedure time (adjusted for patient complexity) were faster at hospitals that kept the original teams intact.

At one hospital where several additional members of the nursing, anesthesiology, and perfusion staff were trained in the new procedure shortly after adoption, the makeup of the team changed with almost every operation. Again and again, teams had to learn from scratch how to work together. After the tenth time, the surgeon demanded a fixed team whenever he performed the new procedure. Operations went more smoothly after that.

FRAMING THE CHALLENGE

When discussing the new procedure with team members, the leaders of teams that successfully implemented the new technology characterized adopting it as an organizational challenge rather than a technical one. They emphasized the importance of creating new ways of working together over simply acquiring new individual skills. They made it clear that this reinvention of working relationships would require the contribution of every team member.

By all accounts, the difficulty of the new procedure makes cardiac surgery even more stressful than usual, at least initially. But many surgeons didn't acknowledge the higher level of stress or help their teams internalize the rationale for taking on this significant new challenge. Instead, they portrayed the technology as a plug-in component in an otherwise unchanged procedure. As one surgeon told us: "I don't see what's really new here. All the basic components of this technology have been around for years." This view led to frustration and resistance among team members. Another surgeon, who characterized the procedure as primarily a technical challenge for surgeons, was assisted by a nurse who, with grim humor, said she would rather slit her wrists than do the new procedure one more time. Her attitude was shared by many we interviewed.

But that attitude wasn't universal. At some hospitals, staff members were excited to be "part of something new," as one expressed it. A nurse reported that she felt honored to be a member of the team, in part because it was "exciting to see patients do so well." The leaders of teams with positive attitudes toward the challenge explicitly acknowledged that the task was difficult and emphasized the importance of each person's contribution. The surgeon who talked of the transfer of pain from the patient to the surgical team helped his team by highlighting, with light humor, the frustration they all faced in this learning challenge.

CREATING AN ENVIRONMENT OF PSYCHOLOGICAL SAFETY

Teams, even more than individuals, learn through trial and error. Because of the many interactions among members, it's very difficult for teams to perform tasks smoothly the first time, despite well-designed training programs and extensive individual preparation. The fastest-learning teams in our study tried different approaches in an effort to shave time from the operation without endangering patients. Indeed, team members uniformly emphasized the importance of experimenting with new ways of doing things to improve team performance—even if some of the new ways turned out not to work.

As we have noted, this learning in action proved to be more effective than the after-action analysis so often touted as key to organizational learning. Real-time learning occasionally yielded insights that might have been lost had a team member waited for a formal review session. During a procedure at one hospital, for instance, a nurse spontaneously suggested solving a surgical problem with a long-discarded type of clamp affectionately known as the "iron intern." The use of the nearly forgotten medical device immediately became part of that team's permanent routine.

When individuals learn, the process of trial and error—propose something, try it, then accept or reject it—occurs in private. But on a team, people risk appearing ignorant or incompetent when they suggest or try something new. This is particularly true in the case of technology implementation, because new technologies often render many of the skills of current "experts" irrelevant. Neutralizing the fear of embarrassment is necessary in order to achieve the robust back-and-forth communication among team members required for real-time learning.

Teams whose members felt comfortable making suggestions, trying things that might not work, pointing out potential problems, and admitting mistakes were more successful in learning the new procedure. By contrast, when people felt uneasy acting this way, the learning process was stifled.

Although the formal training for the new procedure emphasized the need for everyone on the team to speak up with observations, concerns, and questions while using the technology, such feedback often didn't happen. One team member even reported being upbraided for pointing out what he believed to be a life-threatening situation. More typical was the comment of one nurse: "If you observe something that might be a problem, you are obligated to speak up, but you choose your time. I will work around the surgeon and go through his PA [physician's assistant] if there is a problem."

But other teams clearly did foster a sense of psychological safety. How? Through the words and actions of the surgeons who acted as team leaders—not surprising, given the explicit hierarchy of the operating room. At one hospital, the surgeon told team members that they had been selected not only because of their skills but also because of the input they could provide on the process. Another surgeon, according to one of his team members, repeatedly told the team: "I need to hear from you because I'm likely to miss things." The repetition itself was important. If they hear it only once, people tend not to hear—or believe—a message that contradicts old norms.

Leading to Learn

While our research focused on the environment of cardiac surgery, we believe our findings have implications that go well beyond the operating room. Organizations in every industry encounter challenges similar to those faced by our surgical teams. Adopting new technologies or new business processes is highly disruptive, regardless of industry. Like the surgical teams in our study, business teams that use new technology for the first time must deal with a learning curve. And the learning that takes place is not just technical. It is also organizational, with teams confronting problems similar to those encountered by the surgical teams we studied: issues of status and deeply ingrained patterns of communication and behavior.

Implementing an enterprise resource planning system, for example, involves a lot of technical work in configuring databases, setting operational parameters, and ensuring that the software runs properly on a given hardware platform. The hard part for many companies, though, is not the technical side but the fact that ERP systems completely change the dynamics—the team relationships and routines—of the organization. As our study shows, it takes time for teams to learn how decisions should be made and who should talk to whom and when. It takes even longer if people don't feel comfortable speaking up.

There's yet another parallel between business teams and surgical teams. Business teams are often led by people who have been chosen because of their technical skills or expertise in a particular area: Outstanding engineers are selected to lead product development projects, IT experts lead systems implementations, and so on. These experts often find themselves in a position similar to that of the cardiac surgeons. If their teams are to succeed, they must transform themselves from technicians into leaders who can manage teams in such a way that they become learning units.

Thus the key finding of our study—that teams learn more quickly if they are explicitly managed for learning—imposes a significant new burden on many team leaders. Besides maintaining technical expertise, they need to become adept at creating environments for learning. (See "Becoming a Learning Leader" at the end of this article.) This may require them—like surgeons who give up dictatorial authority so that they can function as partners on the operating teams—to shed some of the trappings of their traditional status.

The importance of a team leader's actions suggests that the executives responsible for choosing team leaders need to rethink their own approaches. For instance, if an executive views a team's challenge as purely technical, he or she is more likely to appoint a leader based solely on technical competence. In the worst (and not unfamiliar) case, this can lead to disaster; we've all known superstar technocrats with no interpersonal skills. Clearly, there is a danger in erring too far in the other direction. If team leaders are technically incompetent, they're not only liable to make bad decisions but they also lack the credibility needed to motivate a team. But senior managers need to look beyond technical competence and identify team leaders who can motivate and manage teams of disparate specialists so that they are able to learn the skills and routines needed to succeed.

A New Way to Mend a Broken Heart

THE CARDIAC SURGERY TECHNOLOGY we studied is a modification of conventional cardiac surgery, but it requires the surgical team to take a radical new approach to working together.

The standard cardiac operation has three major phases: opening the chest, stopping the heart, and placing the patient on a heart-lung bypass machine; repairing or replacing damaged coronary arteries or valves; and weaning the patient from bypass and closing the chest wound. The minimally invasive technology, adopted by more than 100 hospitals beginning in the late 1990s, provides an alternative way to gain access to the heart. Instead of cutting through the breastbone, the surgeon uses special equipment to work on the heart through an incision between the ribs.

The small size of the incision changes open-heart surgery in several ways. For one thing, the surgeon has to operate in a severely restricted space. For another, the tubes that connect the patient to the bypass machine must be threaded through an artery and vein in the groin instead of being inserted directly into the heart through the incision. And a tiny catheter with a deflated balloon must be threaded into the aorta, the body's main artery, and the balloon inflated to act as an internal clamp. In conventional cardiac surgery, the aorta is blocked off with external clamps inserted into the open chest.

The placement of the internal clamp is an example of the greater coordination among team members required by the new procedure. Using ultrasound, the anesthesiologist works carefully with the surgeon to monitor the path of the balloon as it is inserted, because the surgeon can't see or feel the catheter. Correct placement is crucial, and the tolerances on balloon location are extremely low. Once the balloon clamp is in position, team members, including the nurse and the perfusionist, must monitor it to be sure it stays in place.

"The pressures have to be monitored on the balloon constantly," said one nurse we interviewed. "The communication with perfusion is critical. When I read the training manual, I couldn't believe it. It was so different from standard cases."

Perhaps it isn't surprising that adoption of the procedure—by all of the teams—took longer than expected. The company that developed the technology estimated that it would take surgical teams about eight operations before they were able to perform the new procedure in the same amount of time as conventional surgery. But for even the fastest-learning teams in our study, the number was closer to 40.

A Tale of Two Hospitals

THE LEADER OF THE TEAM implementing the minimally invasive surgical procedure at Chelsea Hospital was a renowned cardiac surgeon who had significant experience with the new technology. Despite that apparent advantage, his team learned the new procedure more slowly than the teams at many other hospitals, including Mountain Medical Center, where the team leader was a relatively junior surgeon with an interest in trying new techniques. Why?

The new technology as a plug-in component

Chelsea Hospital (the names of the hospitals are pseudonyms) is an urban academic medical center that at the time of our study had just hired a new chief of cardiac surgery. He seemed an ideal choice to lead the department's adoption of the new technology, as he had used the new procedure in numerous operations at another hospital (one that was not in our sample). Administrators at Chelsea supported the surgeon's request to invest in the new technology and agreed to send a team to the supplier company's formal training program.

The surgeon, however, played no role in selecting the team, which was assembled according to seniority. He also didn't participate in the team's dry run prior to the first case. He later explained that he didn't see the technique as particularly challenging, having experimented for years with placing a balloon in the aorta. Consequently, he explained, "it was not a matter of training myself. It was a matter of training the team." Such training, though, wouldn't require a change in his style of communicating with the team, he said: "Once I get the team set up, I never look up [from the operating field]. It's they who have to make sure that everything is flowing."

Mastering the new technology proved unexpectedly difficult for all team members. After almost 50 cases at Chelsea, the surgeon said: "It doesn't seem to be getting that much better. We're a little slicker, but not as slick as I would like to be." As at other sites, team members at Chelsea reported being amazed by the extent to which the procedure imposed a need for a new style and level of communication. But they were less confident than

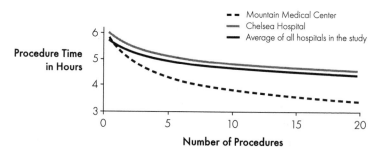

Procedure times have been adjusted for the type of operation and the severity of the patient's illness. The curves are trend lines that reflect the average improvement in procedure times.

team members at other hospitals that they would be able
to put these into practice.

The new technology as a team innovation project

Mountain Medical Center is a respected community hospital serving a small city and the surrounding rural area.
Although the cardiac surgery department didn't have a
history of undertaking major research or cardiac surgical
innovation, it had recently hired a young surgeon who
took an interest in the new procedure. More than any of
the team leaders at other hospitals, this surgeon recognized that implementing the technology would require
the team to adopt a very different style. "The ability of the
surgeon to allow himself to become a partner, not a dic-
tator, is critical," he said. "For example, you really do
have to change what you're doing [during an operation]
based on a suggestion from someone else on the team.
This is a complete restructuring of the [operating room]
and how it works."

Team members, who were picked by the surgeon
based on their experience working together, responded
enthusiastically to his approach. One noted that the "hierarchy [has] changed," creating a "free and open environment with input from everybody." Said another: "I'm
so excited about [the new procedure]. It has been a
model, not just for this hospital but for cardiac surgery. It
is about what a group of people can do." He explained
that the team got better because "the surgeon said,
'Hey, you guys have got to make this thing work.' That's
a great motivator."

In the end, despite the team leader's modest reputation and the hospital's limited experience in implementing
new cardiac procedures, Mountain Medical was one of

the two hospitals in our study that learned the new technology most quickly.

Becoming a Learning Leader

CREATING AN ENVIRONMENT conducive to team learning isn't hard, but it does require a team leader to act quickly. Social psychologists have shown that people watch their supervisors carefully for cues on how team members are expected to behave. These impressions form early in the life of a group or project. To set the right tone, team leaders must:

Be accessible

In order to make clear that others' opinions are welcomed and valued, the leader must be available, not aloof. One nurse in our study commented about a successful team leader: "He's in his office, always just two seconds away. He can always take five minutes to explain something, and he never makes you feel stupid."

Ask for input

An atmosphere of information sharing can be reinforced by an explicit request from the team leader for contributions from members. The surgeon on one successful team "told us to immediately let him know—let everyone know—if anything is out of place," said the team's perfusionist.

Serve as a "fallibility model"

Team leaders can further foster a learning environment by admitting their mistakes to the team. One surgeon in our study explicitly acknowledged his shortcomings.

"He'll say, 'I screwed up. My judgment was bad in that case,'" a team member reported. That signaled to others on the team that errors and concerns could be discussed without fear of punishment.

Originally published in October 2001
Reprint R0109J

What You Don't Know About Making Decisions

DAVID A. GARVIN AND
MICHAEL A. ROBERTO

Executive Summary

MOST EXECUTIVES THINK OF decision making as a sin-
gular event that occurs at a particular point in time. In
reality, though, decision making is a process fraught with
power plays, politics, personal nuances, and institutional
history. Leaders who recognize this make far better decisions than those who persevere in the fantasy that decisions are events they alone control.

That said, some decision-making processes are far
more effective than others. Most often, participants use
an *advocacy* process, possibly the least productive way
to get things done. They view decision making as a contest, arguing passionately for their preferred solutions,
presenting information selectively, withholding relevant
conflicting data so they can make a convincing case,
and standing firm against opposition. Much more powerful is an *inquiry* process, in which people consider a

variety of options and work together to discover the best solution. Moving from advocacy to inquiry requires careful attention to three critical factors: fostering constructive, rather than personal, conflict; making sure everyone knows that their viewpoints are given serious consideration even if they are not ultimately accepted; and knowing when to bring deliberations to a close.

The authors discuss in detail strategies for moving from an advocacy to an inquiry process, as well as for fostering productive conflict, true consideration, and timely closure. And they offer a framework for assessing the effectiveness of your process while you're still in the middle of it.

Decision making is a job that lies at the very heart of leadership and one that requires a genius for balance: the ability to embrace the divergence that may characterize early discussions and to forge the unity needed for effective implementation.

LEADERS SHOW THEIR METTLE in many ways—setting strategy and motivating people, just to mention two—but above all else leaders are made or broken by the quality of their decisions. That's a given, right? If you answered yes, then you would probably be surprised by how many executives approach decision making in a way that neither puts enough options on the table nor permits sufficient evaluation to ensure that they can make the best choice. Indeed, our research over the past several years strongly suggests that, simply put, most leaders get decision making all wrong.

The reason: Most businesspeople treat decision making as an event—a discrete choice that takes place at a single point in time, whether they're sitting at a desk, moderating a meeting, or staring at a spreadsheet. This classic view of decision making has a pronouncement popping out of a leader's head, based on experience, gut, research, or all three. Say the matter at hand is whether to pull a product with weak sales off the market. An "event" leader would mull in solitude, ask for advice, read reports, mull some more, then say yea or nay and send the organization off to make it happen. But to look at decision making that way is to overlook larger social and organizational contexts, which ultimately determine the success of any decision.

The fact is, decision making is not an event. It's a process, one that unfolds over weeks, months, or even years; one that's fraught with power plays and politics and is replete with personal nuances and institutional history; one that's rife with discussion and debate; and one that requires support at all levels of the organization when it comes time for execution. Our research shows that the difference between leaders who make good decisions and those who make bad ones is striking. The former recognize that all decisions are processes, and they explicitly design and manage them as such. The latter persevere in the fantasy that decisions are events they alone control.

In the following pages, we'll explore how leaders can design and manage a sound, effective decision-making process—an approach we call inquiry—and outline a set of criteria for assessing the quality of the decision-making process. First, a look at the process itself.

Decisions as Process: Inquiry Versus Advocacy

Not all decision-making processes are equally effective, particularly in the degree to which they allow a group to identify and consider a wide range of ideas. In our research, we've seen two broad approaches. *Inquiry*, which we prefer, is a very open process designed to generate multiple alternatives, foster the exchange of ideas, and produce a well-tested solution. Unfortunately, this approach doesn't come easily or naturally to most people. Instead, groups charged with making a decision tend to default to the second mode, one we call *advocacy*. The two look deceptively similar on the surface: groups of people, immersed in discussion and debate, trying to select a course of action by drawing on what they believe is the best available evidence. But despite their similarities, inquiry and advocacy produce dramatically different results.

When a group takes an advocacy perspective, participants approach decision making as a contest, although they don't necessarily compete openly or even consciously. Well-defined groups with special interests—dueling divisions in search of budget increases, for example—advocate for particular positions. Participants are passionate about their preferred solutions and therefore stand firm in the face of disagreement. That level of passion makes it nearly impossible to remain objective, limiting people's ability to pay attention to opposing arguments. Advocates often present information selectively, buttressing their arguments while withholding relevant conflicting data. Their goal, after all, is to make a compelling case, not to convey an evenhanded or balanced view. Two different plant managers pushing their own improvement programs, for example, may be wary of reporting potential weak points for fear that full disclosure will jeopardize their chances of winning the debate and gaining access to needed resources.

What's more, the disagreements that arise are frequently fractious and even antagonistic. Personalities and egos come into play, and differences are normally resolved through battles of wills and behind-the-scenes maneuvering. The implicit assumption is that a superior solution will emerge from a test of strength among competing positions. But in fact this approach typically suppresses innovation and encourages participants to go along with the dominant view to avoid further conflict.

By contrast, an inquiry-focused group carefully considers a variety of options and works together to discover the best solution. While people naturally continue to have their own interests, the goal is not to persuade the group to adopt a given point of view but instead to come to agreement on the best course of action. People share information widely, preferably in raw form, to allow participants to draw their own conclusions. Rather than suppressing dissension, an inquiry process encourages critical thinking. All participants feel comfortable raising alternative solutions and asking hard questions about the possibilities already on the table.

People engaged in an inquiry process rigorously question proposals and the assumptions they rest on, so conflict may be intense—but it is seldom personal. In fact, because disagreements revolve around ideas and interpretations rather than entrenched positions, conflict is generally healthy, and team members resolve their differences by applying rules of reason. The implicit assumption is that a consummate solution will emerge from a test of strength among competing ideas rather than dueling positions. Recent accounts of GE's succession process describe board members pursuing just such an open-minded approach. All members met repeatedly with the major candidates and gathered regularly to review their strengths and weaknesses—frequently without Jack Welch in attendance—with little or no attempt to lobby early for a particular choice.

A process characterized by inquiry rather than advocacy tends to produce decisions of higher quality—decisions that not only advance the company's objectives but also are reached in a timely manner and can be implemented effectively. Therefore, we believe that leaders seeking to improve their organizations' decision-making capabilities need to begin with a single goal: moving as quickly as possible from a process of advocacy to one of inquiry. That requires careful attention to three critical factors, the "three C's" of effective decision making: *conflict, consideration,* and *closure*. Each entails a delicate balancing act. See "Two approaches to Decision Making" for more detail.

Constructive Conflict

Critical thinking and rigorous debate invariably lead to conflict. The good news is that conflict brings issues into focus, allowing leaders to make more informed choices. The bad news is that the wrong kind of conflict can derail the decision-making process altogether.

Indeed, conflict comes in two forms—*cognitive* and *affective*. Cognitive, or substantive, conflict relates to the work at hand. It involves disagreements over ideas and assumptions and differing views on the best way to proceed. Not only is such conflict healthy, it's crucial to effective inquiry. When people express differences openly and challenge underlying assumptions, they can flag real weaknesses and introduce new ideas. Affective, or interpersonal, conflict is emotional. It involves personal friction, rivalries, and clashing personalities, and it tends to diminish people's willingness to cooperate during implementation, rendering the decision-making process less effective. Not surprisingly, it is a common feature of advocacy processes.

On examination, the two are easy to distinguish. When a team member recalls "tough debates about the strategic, financial, and operating merits of the three acquisition candidates," she is referring to cognitive conflict. When a team member comments on "heated arguments that degenerated into personal attacks," he means affective conflict. But in practice the two types of conflict are surprisingly hard to separate. People tend to take any criticism personally and react defensively. The

Two Approaches to Decision Making

	Advocacy	Inquiry
Concept of Decision Making	A contest	Collaborative problem solving
Purpose of Discussion	Persuasion and lobbying	Testing and evaluation
Participants' Role	Spokespeople	Critical thinkers
Patterns of Behavior	Strive to persuade others	Present balanced arguments
	Defend your position	Remain open to alternatives
	Downplay weaknesses	Accept constructive criticism
Minority Views	Discouraged or dismissed	Cultivated and valued
Outcome	Winners and losers	Collective ownership

atmosphere quickly becomes charged, and even if a high-quality decision emerges, the emotional fallout tends to linger, making it hard for team members to work together during implementation.

The challenge for leaders is to increase cognitive conflict while keeping affective conflict low—no mean feat. One technique is to establish norms that make vigorous debate the rule rather than the exception. Chuck Knight, for 27 years the CEO of Emerson Electric, accomplished this by relentlessly grilling managers during planning reviews, no matter what he actually thought of the proposal on the table, asking tough, combative questions and expecting well-framed responses. The process—which Knight called the "logic of illogic" because of his willingness to test even well-crafted arguments by raising unexpected, and occasionally fanciful, concerns—was undoubtedly intimidating. But during his tenure it produced a steady stream of smart investment decisions and an unbroken string of quarterly increases in net income.

Bob Galvin, when he was CEO of Motorola in the 1980s, took a slightly different approach. He habitually asked unexpected hypothetical questions that stimulated creative thinking. Subsequently, as chairman of the board of overseers for the Malcolm Baldrige National Quality Program, Galvin took his colleagues by surprise when, in response to pressure from constituents to broaden the criteria for the award, he proposed narrowing them instead. In the end, the board did in fact broaden the criteria, but his seemingly out-of-the-blue suggestion sparked a creative and highly productive debate.

Another technique is to structure the conversation so that the process, by its very nature, fosters debate. This can be done by dividing people into groups with different, and often competing, responsibilities. For example, one group may be asked to develop a proposal while the other generates alternative recommendations. Then the groups would exchange proposals and discuss the various options. Such techniques virtually guarantee high levels of cognitive conflict. (The exhibit "Structuring the Debate" outlines two approaches for using different groups to stimulate creative thinking.)

But even if you've structured the process with an eye toward encouraging cognitive conflict, there's always a risk that it will become personal. Beyond cooling the debate with "time-outs," skilled leaders use a number of creative techniques to elevate cognitive debate while minimizing affective conflict.

First, adroit leaders pay careful attention to the way issues are framed, as well as to the language used during discussions. They preface contradictory remarks or questions with phrases that remove some of the personal sting ("Your arguments make good sense, but let me play devil's advocate for a moment"). They also set ground rules about language, insisting that team members avoid words and behavior that trigger defensiveness. For instance, in the U.S. Army's after-action reviews, conducted immediately after missions to identify mistakes so they can be avoided next time, facilitators make a point of saying, "We don't use the 'b' word, and we don't use the 'f' word. We don't place blame, and we don't find fault."

Second, leaders can help people step back from their preestablished positions by breaking up natural coalitions and assigning people to tasks on some basis other than traditional loyalties. At a leading aerospace company, one business unit president had to deal with two

Structuring the Debate

By breaking a decision-making body into two subgroups, leaders can often create an environment in which people feel more comfortable engaging in debate. Scholars recommend two techniques in particular, which we call the "point-counterpoint" and "intellectual watchdog" approaches. The first three steps are the same for both techniques:

Point-Counterpoint	Intellectual Watchdog
The team divides into two subgroups.	The team divides into two subgroups.
Subgroup A develops a proposal, fleshing out the recommendation, the key assumptions, and the critical supporting data.	Subgroup A develops a proposal, fleshing out the recommendation, the key assumptions, and the critical supporting data.
Subgroup A presents the proposal to Subgroup B in written and oral forms.	Subgroup A presents the proposal to Subgroup B in written and oral forms.
Subgroup B generates one or more alternative plans of action.	Subgroup B develops a detailed critique of these assumptions and recommendations. It presents this critique in written and oral forms. Subgroup A revises its proposal based on this feedback.
The subgroups come together to debate the proposals and seek agreement on a common set of assumptions.	The subgroups continue in this revision-critique-revision cycle until they converge on a common set of assumptions.
Based on those assumptions, the subgroups continue to debate various options and strive to agree on a common set of recommendations.	Then, the subgroups work together to develop a common set of recommendations.

powerful coalitions within his organization during a critical decision about entering into a strategic alliance. When he set up two groups to consider alternative alliance partners, he interspersed the groups with members of each coalition, forcing people with different interests to work with one another. He then asked both groups to evaluate the same wide range of options using different criteria (such as technological capability, manufacturing prowess, or project management skills). The two groups then shared their evaluations and worked together to select the best partner. Because nobody had complete information, they were forced to listen closely to one another.

Third, leaders can shift individuals out of well-grooved patterns, where vested interests are highest. They can, for example, ask team members to research and argue for a position they did not endorse during initial discussions. Similarly, they can assign team members to play functional or managerial roles different from their own, such as asking an operations executive to take the marketing view or asking a lower-level employee to assume the CEO's strategic perspective.

Finally, leaders can ask participants locked in debate to revisit key facts and assumptions and gather more information. Often, people become so focused on the differences between opposing positions that they reach a stalemate. Emotional conflict soon follows. Asking people to examine underlying presumptions can defuse the tension and set the team back on track. For instance, at Enron, when people disagree strongly about whether or not to apply their trading skills to a new commodity or market, senior executives quickly refocus the discussion on characteristics of industry structure and assumptions about market size and customer preferences. People quickly recognize areas of agreement, discover precisely how and why they disagree, and then focus their debate on specific issues.

Consideration

Once a decision's been made and the alternatives dismissed, some people will have to surrender the solution they preferred. At times, those who are overruled resist the outcome; at other times, they display grudging acceptance. What accounts for the difference? The critical factor appears to be the perception of fairness—what scholars call "procedural justice." The reality is that the leader will make the ultimate decision, but the people participating in the process must believe that their views were considered and that they had a genuine opportunity to influence the final decision. Researchers have found that if participants believe the process was fair, they are far more willing to commit themselves to the resulting decision even if their views did not prevail.

Many managers equate fairness with *voice*—with giving everyone a chance to express his or her own views. They doggedly work their way around the table, getting everyone's input. However, voice is not nearly as important as *consideration*—people's belief that the leader actively listened to them during the discussions and weighed their views carefully before reaching a decision. In his 1999 book, *Only the Paranoid Survive*, Intel's chairman Andy Grove describes how he explains the distinction to his middle managers: "Your criterion for involvement should be that you're heard and understood. . . . All sides cannot prevail in the debate, but all opinions have value in shaping the right answer."

In fact, voice without consideration is often damaging; it leads to resentment and frustration rather than to acceptance. When the time comes to implement the decision, people are likely to drag their feet if they sense that the decision-making process had been a sham—an exercise in going through the motions designed to validate the leader's preferred solution. This appears to have been true of the Daimler-Chrysler merger. Daimler CEO Jurgen Schrempp asked for extensive analysis and assessment of potential merger candidates but had long before settled on Chrysler as his choice. In fact, when consultants told him that his strategy was unlikely to create shareholder value, he dismissed the data and went ahead with his plans. Schrempp may have solicited views from many parties, but he clearly failed to give them much weight.

Leaders can demonstrate consideration throughout the decision-making process. At the outset, they need to convey openness to new ideas and a willingness to accept views that differ from their own. In particular, they must avoid suggesting that their minds are already made up. They should avoid disclosing their personal preferences early in the process, or they should clearly state that any initial opinions are provisional and subject to change. Or they can absent themselves from early deliberations.

During the discussions, leaders must take care to show that they are listening actively and attentively. How? By asking questions, probing for deeper explanations, echoing comments, making eye contact, and showing patience when participants explain their positions. Taking notes is an especially powerful signal, since it suggests that the leader is making a real effort to capture, understand, and evaluate people's thoughts.

And after they make the final choice, leaders should explain their logic. They must describe the rationale for their decision, detailing the criteria they used to select a course of action. Perhaps more important, they need to convey how each participant's arguments affected the final decision or explain clearly why they chose to differ with those views.

Closure

Knowing when to end deliberations is tricky; all too often decision-making bodies rush to a conclusion or else dither endlessly and decide too late. Deciding too early is as damaging as deciding too late, and both problems can usually be traced to unchecked advocacy.

DECIDING TOO EARLY

Sometimes people's desire to be considered team players overrides their willingness to engage in critical thinking and thoughtful analysis, so the group readily accepts the first remotely plausible option. Popularly known as "groupthink," this mind-set is prevalent in the presence of strong advocates, especially in new teams, whose members are still learning the rules and may be less willing to stand out as dissenters.

The danger of groupthink is not only that it suppresses the full range of options but also that unstated objections will come to the surface at some critical moment—usually at a time when aligned, cooperative action is essential to implementation. The leader of a large division of a fast-growing retailer learned this the hard way. He liked to work with a small subset of his senior team to generate options, evaluate the alternatives, and develop a plan of action, and then bring the proposal back to the full team for validation. At that point, his managers would feel they had been presented with a fait accompli and so would be reluctant to raise their concerns. As one of them put it: "Because the meeting is the wrong place to object, we don't walk out of the room as a unified group." Instead, they would reopen the debate during implementation, delaying important initiatives by many months.

As their first line of defense against groupthink, leaders need to learn to recognize latent discontent, paying special attention to body language: furrowed brows, crossed arms, or curled-up defiance. To bring disaffected people back into the discussion, it may be best to call for a break, approach dissenters one by one, encourage them to speak up, and then reconvene. GM's Alfred Sloan was famous for this approach, which he would introduce with the following speech: "I take it we are all in complete agreement on the decision here. Then I propose we postpone further discussion of the matter until our next meeting to give ourselves time to develop disagreement and perhaps gain some understanding of what the decision is all about."

Another way to avoid early closure is to cultivate minority views either through norms or through explicit rules. Minority views broaden and deepen debate; they stretch a group's thinking, even though they are seldom adopted intact. It is for this reason that Andy Grove routinely seeks input from "helpful Cassandras," people who are known for raising hard questions and offering fresh perspectives about the dangers of proposed policies.

DECIDING TOO LATE

Here, too, unchecked advocacy is frequently the source of the problem, and in these instances it takes two main forms. At times, a team hits gridlock: Warring factions refuse to yield, restating their positions over and over again. Without a mechanism for breaking the deadlock, discussions become an endless loop. At other times, people bend over backward to ensure evenhanded participation. Striving for fairness, team members insist on hearing every view and resolving every question before reaching a conclusion. This demand for certainty—for complete arguments backed by unassailable data—is its own peculiar form of advocacy. Once again, the result is usually an endless loop, replaying the same alternatives, objections, and requests for further information. Any member of the group can unilaterally derail the discussion by voicing doubts. Meanwhile, competitive pressures may be demanding an immediate response, or participants may have tuned out long ago, as the same arguments are repeated ad nauseam.

At this point, it's the leader's job to "call the question." Jamie Houghton, the longtime CEO of Corning, invented a vivid metaphor to describe this role. He spoke of wearing two hats when working with his senior team: He figuratively put on his cowboy hat when he wanted to debate with members as an equal, and he donned a bowler when, as CEO, he called the question and announced a decision. The former role allowed for challenges and continued discussion; the latter signaled an end to the debate.

The message here is that leaders—and their teams—need to become more comfortable with ambiguity and be willing to make speedy decisions in the absence of complete, unequivocal data or support. As Dean Stanley Teele of Harvard Business School was fond of telling students: "The art of management is the art of making meaningful generalizations out of inadequate facts."

A Litmus Test

Unfortunately, superior decision making is distressingly difficult to assess in real time. Successful outcomes—decisions of high quality, made in a timely manner and implemented effectively—can be evaluated only after the fact. But by the time the results are in, it's normally too late to take corrective action. Is there any way to find out earlier whether you're on the right track?

There is indeed. The trick, we believe, is to periodically assess the decision-making process, even as it is under way. Scholars now have considerable evidence showing that a small set of process traits is closely linked with superior outcomes. While they are no guarantee of success, their combined presence sharply improves the odds that you'll make a good decision.

MULTIPLE ALTERNATIVES

When groups consider many alternatives, they engage in more thoughtful analysis and usually avoid settling too quickly on the easy, obvious answer. This is one reason techniques like point-counterpoint, which requires groups to generate at least two alternatives, are so often associated with superior decision making. Usually, keeping track of the number of options being considered will tell if this test has been met. But take care not to double count. Go-no-go choices involve only one option and don't qualify as two alternatives.

ASSUMPTION TESTING

"Facts" come in two varieties: those that have been carefully tested and those that have been merely asserted or

assumed. Effective decision-making groups do not confuse the two. They periodically step back from their arguments and try to confirm their assumptions by examin-
ing them critically. If they find that some still lack hard
evidence, they may elect to proceed, but they will at least
know they're venturing into uncertain territory. Alterna-
tively, the group may designate "intellectual watchdogs"
who are assigned the task of scrutinizing the process
for unchecked assumptions and challenging them on
the spot.

WELL-DEFINED CRITERIA

Without crisp, clear goals, it's easy to fall into the trap of
comparing apples with oranges. Competing arguments
become difficult to judge, since advocates will suggest
using those measures (net income, return on capital,
market presence, share of mind, and so on) that favor
their preferred alternative. Fuzzy thinking and long
delays are the likely result.

To avoid the problem, the team should specify goals
up front and revisit them repeatedly during the decision-
making process. These goals can be complex and multi-
faceted, quantitative and qualitative, but whatever form
they take, they must remain at the fore. Studies of
merger decisions have found that as the process reaches
its final stages and managers feel the pressure of deadlines and the rush to close, they often compromise or
adjust the criteria they originally created for judging the
appropriateness of the deal.

DISSENT AND DEBATE

David Hume, the great Scottish philosopher, argued per-
suasively for the merits of debate when he observed that

the "truth springs from arguments amongst friends."
There are two ways to measure the health of a debate:
the kinds of questions being asked and the level of
listening.

Some questions open up discussion; others narrow it
and end deliberations. Contrarian hypothetical questions
usually trigger healthy debate. A manager who worked
for former American Express CEO Harvey Golub points
to a time when the company was committed to lowering
credit card fees, and Golub unexpectedly proposed raising fees instead. "I don't think he meant it seriously,"
says the manager. "But he certainly taught us how to
think about fees."

The level of listening is an equally important indicator
of a healthy decision-making process. Poor listening produces flawed analysis as well as personal friction. If participants routinely interrupt one another or pile on
rebuttals before digesting the preceding comment, affective conflict is likely to materialize. Civilized discussions
quickly become impossible, for collegiality and group
harmony usually disappear in the absence of active
listening.

PERCEIVED FAIRNESS

A real-time measure of perceived fairness is the level of
participation that's maintained after a key midpoint or
milestone has been reached. Often, a drop in participation is an early warning of problems with implementation since some members of the group are already showing their displeasure by voting with their feet.

In fact, keeping people involved in the process is, in
the end, perhaps the most crucial factor in making a
decision—and making it stick. It's a job that lies at the
heart of leadership and one that uniquely combines the

leader's numerous talents. It requires the fortitude to promote conflict while accepting ambiguity, the wisdom to know when to bring conversations to a close, the patience to help others understand the reasoning behind your choice, and, not least, a genius for balance—the ability to embrace both the divergence that may characterize early discussions and the unity needed for effective implementation. Cyrus the Great, the founder of the Persian Empire and a renowned military leader, understood the true hallmark of leadership in the sixth century BC, when he attributed his success to "diversity in counsel, unity in command."

Advocacy Versus Inquiry in Action: The Bay of Pigs and the Cuban Missile Crisis

PERHAPS THE BEST DEMONSTRATION of advocacy versus inquiry comes from the administration of President John F. Kennedy. During his first two years in office, Kennedy wrestled with two critical foreign policy decisions: the Bay of Pigs invasion and the Cuban Missile Crisis. Both were assigned to cabinet-level task forces, involving many of the same players, the same political interests, and extremely high stakes. But the results were extraordinarily different, largely because the two groups operated in different modes.

The first group, charged with deciding whether to support an invasion of Cuba by a small army of U.S.-trained Cuban exiles, worked in advocacy mode, and the outcome is widely regarded as an example of flawed decision making. Shortly after taking office, President Kennedy learned of the planned attack on Cuba developed by the CIA during the Eisenhower administration. Backed by the Joint Chiefs of Staff, the CIA argued forcefully for the invasion and minimized the risks, filtering the information presented to the president to reinforce the agency's position. Knowledgeable individuals on the State Department's Latin America desk were excluded from deliberations because of their likely opposition.

Some members of Kennedy's staff opposed the plan but held their tongues for fear of appearing weak in the face of strong advocacy by the CIA. As a result, there was little debate, and the group failed to test some critical underlying assumptions. For example, they didn't question whether the landing would in fact lead to a rapid domestic uprising against Castro, and they failed to find out whether the exiles could fade into the mountains (which were 80 miles from the landing site) should they meet with strong resistance. The resulting invasion is generally considered to be one of the low points of the Cold War. About 100 lives were lost, and the rest of the exiles were taken hostage. The incident was a major embarrassment to the Kennedy administration and dealt a blow to America's global standing.

After the botched invasion, Kennedy conducted a review of the foreign policy decision-making process and introduced five major changes, essentially transforming the process into one of inquiry. First, people were urged to participate in discussions as "skeptical generalists"— that is, as disinterested critical thinkers rather than as representatives of particular departments. Second, Robert Kennedy and Theodore Sorensen were assigned the role of intellectual watchdog, expected to pursue every possible point of contention, uncovering weaknesses and untested assumptions. Third, task forces were urged to abandon the rules of protocol, eliminating formal agendas and deference to rank. Fourth, participants were expected to split occasionally into subgroups to develop a broad range of options. And finally, President Kennedy decided to absent himself from some of the early task force meetings to avoid influencing other participants and slanting the debate.

The inquiry mode was used to great effect when in October 1962 President Kennedy learned that the Soviet Union had placed nuclear missiles on Cuban soil, despite repeated assurances from the Soviet ambassador that this would not occur. Kennedy immediately convened a high-level task force, which contained many of the same men responsible for the Bay of Pigs invasion, and asked them to frame a response. The group met night and day for two weeks, often inviting additional members to join in their deliberations to broaden their perspective. Occasionally, to encourage the free flow of ideas, they met without the president. Robert Kennedy played his new role thoughtfully, critiquing options frequently and encouraging the group to develop additional alternatives. In particular, he urged the group to move beyond a simple go-no-go decision on a military air strike.

Ultimately, subgroups developed two positions, one favoring a blockade and the other an air strike. These groups gathered information from a broad range of sources, viewed and interpreted the same intelligence photos, and took great care to identify and test underlying assumptions, such as whether the Tactical Air Command was indeed capable of eliminating all Soviet missiles in a surgical air strike. The subgroups exchanged position papers, critiqued each other's proposals, and came together to debate the alternatives. They presented Kennedy with both options, leaving him to make the final choice. The result was a carefully framed response, leading to a successful blockade and a peaceful end to the crisis.

Originally published in September 2001
Reprint R0108G

Communities of Practice

The Organizational Frontier

ETIENNE C. WENGER AND
WILLIAM M. SNYDER

Executive Summary

A NEW ORGANIZATIONAL FORM is emerging in companies that run on knowledge: the community of practice. And for this expanding universe of companies, communities of practice promise to radically galvanize knowledge sharing, learning, and change.

A community of practice is a group of people informally bound together by shared expertise and passion for a joint enterprise. People in companies form them for a variety of reasons—to maintain connections with peers when the company reorganizes; to respond to external changes such as the rise of e-commerce; or to meet new challenges when the company changes strategy.

Regardless of the circumstances that give rise to communities of practice, their members inevitably share knowledge in free-flowing, creative ways that foster new approaches to problems. Over the past five years, the authors have seen communities of practice improve performance at companies as diverse as an international bank, a major car manufacturer, and a U.S. government agency. Communities of practice can drive strategy, generate new lines of business, solve problems, promote the spread of best practices, develop people's skills, and help companies recruit and retain talent.

The paradox of such communities is that although they are self-organizing and thus resistant to supervision and interference, they do not require specific managerial efforts to develop them and integrate them into an organization. Only then can they be fully leveraged.

The authors explain the steps managers need to take in order to get communities going—and to sustain them so they can become a central part of their companies' success.

Today's economy runs on knowledge, and most companies work assiduously to capitalize on that fact. They use cross-functional teams, customer- or product-focused business units, and work groups—to name just a few organizational forms—to capture and spread ideas and know-how. In many cases, these ways of organizing are very effective, and no one would argue for their demise. But a new organizational form is emerging that promises to complement existing structures and radically galvanize knowledge sharing, learning, and change. It's called the community of practice.

What are communities of practice? In brief, they're groups of people informally bound together by shared expertise and passion for a joint enterprise—engineers engaged in deep-water drilling, for example, consultants who specialize in strategic marketing, or frontline managers in charge of check processing at a large commercial bank. Some communities of practice meet regularly—for lunch on Thursdays, say. Others are connected primarily by e-mail networks. A community of practice may or may not have an explicit agenda on a given week, and even if it does, it may not follow the agenda closely. Inevitably, however, people in communities of practice share their experiences and knowledge in free-flowing, creative ways that foster new approaches to problems.

Because its primary "output"—knowledge—is intangible, the community of practice might sound like another "soft" management fad. But that's not the case. During the past five years, we have seen communities of practice improve organizational performance at companies as diverse as an international bank, a major car manufacturer, and a U.S. government agency. Communities of practice can drive strategy, generate new lines of business, solve problems, promote the spread of best practices, develop people's professional skills, and help companies recruit and retain talent. (For examples of how communities of practice have helped companies, see "Communities in Action" at the end of this article.)

If communities of practice are so effective, why aren't they more prevalent? There are three reasons. The first is that although communities of practice have been around for a long time—for centuries, in fact—the term has just recently entered the business vernacular. The second is that only several dozen forward-thinking companies have taken the leap of "installing" or nurturing them. The third reason is that it's not particularly easy to build and sustain communities of practice or to integrate them with the rest of an organization. The organic, spontaneous, and informal nature of communities of practice makes them resistant to supervision and interference.

But we have observed a number of companies that have overcome the managerial paradox inherent in communities of practice and successfully nurtured them. In general, we have found that managers cannot mandate communities of practice. Instead, successful managers bring the right people together, provide an infrastructure in which communities can thrive, and measure the communities' value in nontraditional ways. These tasks of cultivation aren't easy, but the harvest they yield makes them well worth the effort.

The Hallmarks of Communities of Practice

Communities of practice were common as far back as ancient times. In classical Greece, for instance, "corporations" of metalworkers, potters, masons, and other craftsmen had both a social purpose (members worshiped the same deities and celebrated holidays together) and a business function (members trained apprentices and spread innovations). In the Middle Ages, guilds played similar roles for artisans throughout Europe. Today's communities of practice are different in one important respect: instead of being composed primarily of people working on their own, they often exist within large organizations.

Communities of practice are as diverse as the situations that give rise to them. People in companies form them for a variety of reasons. For example, when a company reorganizes into a team-based structure, employees with functional expertise may create communities of practice as a way of maintaining connections with peers.

Elsewhere, people may form communities in response to changes originating outside the organization, such as the rise of e-commerce, or inside, such as new company strategies—think of auto manufacturers going into the financing business or computer makers offering consulting services.

A community of practice can exist entirely within a business unit or stretch across divisional boundaries. A community can even thrive with members from different companies; for example, the CEOs who make up the Business Roundtable meet regularly to discuss relationships between business and public policy, among other things. A community can be made up of tens or even hundreds of people, but typically it has a core of participants whose passion for the topic energizes the community and who provide intellectual and social leadership. Large communities are often subdivided by geographic region or by subject matter in order to encourage people to take part actively.

Communities of practice differ from other forms of organization in several ways. (For a summary of the differences, see the exhibit "A Snapshot Comparison.") Consider, briefly, how communities differ from teams. Teams are created by managers to complete specific projects. Managers select team members on the basis of their ability to contribute to the team's goals, and the group disbands once the project has been finished. Communities of practice, on the other hand, are informal—they organize themselves, meaning they set their own agendas and establish their own leadership. And membership in a community of practice is self-selected. In other words, people in such communities tend to know when and if they should join. They know if they have something to give and whether they are likely to take

A Snapshot Comparison

Communities of practice, formal work groups, teams, and informal networks are useful in complementary ways. Below is a summary of their characteristics.

	What's the Purpose?	Who Belongs?	What Holds It Together?	How Long Does It Last?
Community of Practice	To develop members' capabilities; to build and exchange knowledge	Members who select themselves	Passion, commitment, and identification with the group's expertise	As long as there is interest in maintaining the group
Formal Work Group	To deliver a product or service	Everyone who reports to the group's manager	Job requirements and common goals	Until the next reorganization
Project Team	To accomplish a specified task	Employees assigned by senior management	The project's milestones and goals	Until the project has been completed
Informal Network	To collect and pass on business information	Friends and business acquaintances	Mutual needs	As long as people have a reason to connect

something away. And members of an existing community, when they invite someone to join, also operate on a gut sense of the prospective member's appropriateness for the group.

To get a better sense of how communities of practice look in action, let's consider two examples.

At the Hill's Pet Nutrition facility in Richmond, Indiana, line technicians meet weekly to talk about recent successes and frustrations as well as challenges looming ahead. They formed the group several years ago after managers and technicians attended a retreat where they were introduced to the concept of communities of practice and learned how such groups could help the company develop and retain technical expertise. The group has a "mayor" who's been chosen by his peers to keep things on track from week to week and see to it that people with relevant expertise are present when needed. The plant grants people time to participate. Actual attendance fluctuates depending on the agenda.

At a recent gathering we observed, 12 technicians from the first and second shifts met around a large table in the glass-walled conference room overlooking the plant. Although it was midafternoon, they were soon joined by Roger, a technician from the third shift who would have to return seven hours later to begin his "real" work. Roger made a special trip in on this occasion to help John hone his proposal to substitute pneumatic tubes for the balky conveyor belt that carried the pet food kibbles to the packaging bin; Roger's background in plumbing was thus particularly relevant.

Senior managers at the plant had not warmed to the pneumatic tube idea. They believed the conveyor system would work if people just operated it properly. They felt the new approach was unproven and, in any case, would be difficult to incorporate with the plant's current technology. Nevertheless, community members had encouraged John to continue pushing for change, and John had pressed on, buoyed by the knowledge that experts in his community of practice saw merit in his proposal.

Before the group members took up John's proposal, they followed their usual opening routine—going around the table and letting people vent about one thing or another, including the most recent Colts game. They also followed up on the previous week's discussion about rethinking how new technicians are certified. Then they turned to the proposal.

Vince began by reviewing management's concerns. John then explained that the latest revision of his proposal included evidence from colleagues in other plants that the technology was reliable and would be compatible with existing equipment. Roger was able to confirm the evidence based on his own experience and suggested that he go along the next time John presented his ideas to management.

The community support for John's work ultimately paid off. A year after the meeting, the company installed the new technology. The result? Significant reductions in downtime and wasted pet food related to packaging. In addition to benefiting the company in this way, the community provides important benefits for members: it gives them opportunities to solve nagging problems and hone their ability to run the plant effectively. Improvements in operations can lead to financial rewards in the form of bonuses that are tied to the plant's performance.

Our second example comes from Hewlett-Packard, where a community of practice consisting of product-delivery consultants from around North America holds monthly teleconferences. The community focuses on an HP software product called High Availability, which minimizes computer downtime for customers. The core group of consultants, who had been somewhat isolated, came together a few years ago with the help of facilitators from a knowledge management support team. The members discovered that they had many problems in common and that they could learn a great deal from one another. The community has succeeded in standardizing the software's sales and installation processes and establishing a consistent pricing scheme for HP salespeople.

Participation in the monthly calls is voluntary, but levels of attendance are steady. For one such call, the focus was meant to be on Maureen's experiences with a major customer for which she was installing the product. Before diving in, however, the consultants spent the first ten minutes chatting about the recent reorganization of their division—whether it was a good thing, what it meant for them, and so on.

Maureen hadn't spent a lot of time preparing a formal presentation; she knew that only by talking directly and openly could she spur the give-and-take that would make the call worthwhile for the group. As the call proceeded, community members interrupted her constantly with questions and examples from their own experiences—all of which helped Maureen understand how to work more effectively with her clients.

The conversation then turned to a persistent bug in the software. Rob, a member of the software division that developed the product, had been invited to take part in these calls to create a stronger connection between the product-delivery consultants and software developers. He'd already worked out a way to get rid of the bug, but he learned from the stories he heard in the teleconference how to make the fix even more effective. He told the group that he would follow up during next month's call.

The participants in these communities of practice were learning together by focusing on problems that were directly related to their work. In the short term, this made their work easier or more effective; in the long term, it helped build both their communities and their shared practices—thus developing capabilities critical to the continuing success of the organizations.

The strength of communities of practice is self-perpetuating. As they generate knowledge, they reinforce and renew themselves. That's why communities of practice give you not only the golden eggs but also the goose that lays them. The farmer killed the goose to get all the gold and ended up losing both; the challenge for organizations is to appreciate the goose and to understand how to keep it alive and productive.

A Paradox of Management

Although communities of practice are fundamentally informal and self-organizing, they benefit from cultivation. Like gardens, they respond to attention that respects their nature. You can't tug on a cornstalk to make it grow faster or taller, and you shouldn't yank a marigold out of the ground to see if it has roots. You can, however, till the soil, pull out weeds, add water during dry spells, and ensure that your plants have the proper nutrients. And while you may welcome the wildflowers that bloom without any cultivation, you may get even more satisfaction from those vegetables and flowers you started from seed.

The same is true for companies that grow communities of practice from seed. To get communities going—and to sustain them over time—managers should:

- identify potential communities of practice that will enhance the company's strategic capabilities;

- provide the infrastructure that will support such communities and enable them to apply their expertise effectively;

- use nontraditional methods to assess the value of the company's communities of practice.

IDENTIFYING POTENTIAL COMMUNITIES

Communities of practice should not be created in a vacuum. In most cases, informal networks of people with the ability and the passion to further develop an organization's core competencies already exist. The task is to identify such groups and help them come together as communities of practice. At Shell, for example, a person who wants to develop a new community joins forces with a consultant and interviews prospective members. They look at challenges and problems that people across units and teams have in common and that would serve as bases for a community of practice. The interviews are not only a means of collecting information; they also generate enthusiasm for the embryonic community. After laying the groundwork, the coordinator calls the members of the community of practice together, and the group begins discussing plans for activities that will build individual and group capabilities and advance the company's strategic agenda.

A key task is defining a community's domain. If members don't feel personally connected to the group's area of expertise and interest once it has been defined, they won't fully commit themselves to the work of the community. The U.S. Veterans Administration found this to be true with a community it started in its claims-processing organization. The core group first defined its focus as "technical capability," an umbrella term covering employees' processing skills and the associated procedures and equipment. During the community's first year, the core group's participation was limited and progress was slow. The more active members decided they could move faster if they redefined the community's domain. They created subcommunities of first-line managers, customer service representatives, and training coordinators. As a result, the first-line managers are sharing tips about implementing a new team structure, the customer service reps are helping to set standards to reduce processing time, and the training coordinators are upgrading training modules across the organization.

PROVIDING THE INFRASTRUCTURE

Communities of practice are vulnerable because they lack the legitimacy—and the budgets—of established departments. To reach their full potential, then, they need to be integrated into the business and supported in specific ways.

Senior executives must be prepared to invest time and money in helping such communities reach their full potential. That means intervening when communities run up against obstacles to their progress, such as IT systems that don't serve them, promotion systems that overlook community contributions, and reward structures that discourage collaboration. It also means linking communities to related initiatives such as a corporate university.

One way to strengthen communities of practice is to provide them with official sponsors and support teams. Such sponsors and teams do not design the communities or prescribe their activities or outcomes. Instead, they work with internal community leaders to provide resources and coordination.

Companies have done this using a range of approaches. Compare the cases of two organizations— American Management Systems (AMS) and the World Bank—each of which has adopted the community of practice as the foundation of its knowledge management strategy. AMS takes an especially formal approach, while the World Bank combines formal and informal methods. A few years ago, AMS was going through an intense period of growth and globalization and, as a result, was losing its distinctive ability to leverage knowledge across the company. Then-chairman Charles Rossotti personally invited "thought leaders," who had been nominated by their business units, to spearhead the development of communities of practice in strategic areas. The company pays for two to three weeks of the leaders' time each year for these activities.

Community membership at AMS is a privilege. To join a community, a potential member must be recognized as an expert by his or her manager. Once on board, a participant has to complete one knowledge-development project per year—for instance, documenting a best practice—in order to remain in the community. Community members' participation is paid for by their business units, which fund their annual projects, cover their attendance at workshops, and send them to an annual conference that brings together all the company's communities of practice.

At the World Bank, president James Wolfensohn established the goal of making his organization the "knowledge bank"—a global source for high-quality information on economic development—so that it could better fulfill its mission of eradicating poverty. Key people throughout the organization then took the initiative to start communities of practice. Membership is open, and members decide on the level of participation that suits their needs. Communities of practice receive funding for specific activities and manage their own budgets.

At both AMS and the World Bank, senior management boards sponsor communities. Support teams help with community development and coordinate annual community conferences, knowledge fairs, library services, and technical support. Both organizations also have started to fund positions for knowledge managers who assist community leaders. These facilitators coordinate the groups, organize events, respond to queries from members, and keep the communities current on information from external sources.

AMS is exploring ways of explicitly rewarding community members. It has a promotion system that formally acknowledges their work, and it grants nonfinancial rewards such as early access to innovative technology and special business cards that attest to the members' expertise. The World Bank also formally recognizes community participation through its personnel evaluation system, but to drive participation it relies primarily on the intrinsic benefits of community membership: the opportunities to solve problems, develop new ideas, and build relationships with peers who share a common passion.

At both AMS and the World Bank, communities of practice have brought together people and ideas, and they have spread knowledge throughout the companies' global operations. They have made demonstrable and significant contributions to the organizations' goals. These two cases show how different styles of formal commitment to communities of practice by senior managers can be very effective when aligned with the organization's culture.

USING NONTRADITIONAL METHODS TO MEASURE VALUE

Leaders intuitively recognize the benefit of developing people's capabilities. That said, most have difficulty understanding the value of communities. For one thing, the effects of community activities are often delayed. For another, results generally appear in the work of teams and business units, not in the communities themselves. And it's often hard to determine whether a great idea that surfaced during a community meeting would have bubbled up anyway in a different setting. Such complexity makes it very difficult for managers to assess the value of communities.

The best way for an executive to assess the value of a community of practice is by listening to members' stories, which can clarify the complex relationships among activities, knowledge, and performance. "The idea we pursued at that meeting helped me persuade the customer to continue to buy our service." "Thanks to advice from the community, I got done in two days what normally takes me two weeks." "I took a risk because I was confident I had the backing of my community—and it paid off."

The solution to the conundrum of valuing communities of practice is to gather anecdotal evidence systematically. You can't just collect certain stories, perhaps the most compelling ones, because isolated events can be unrepresentative. A systematic effort captures the diversity and range of activities that communities are involved in.

At Shell, community coordinators often conduct interviews to collect these stories and then publish them in newsletters and reports. AMS organizes a yearly competition to identify the best stories. An analysis of a sample of stories revealed that the communities had saved the company $2 million to $5 million and increased revenue by more than $13 million in one year.

The New Frontier

Communities of practice are emerging in companies that thrive on knowledge. The first step for managers now is to understand what these communities are and how they work. The second step is to realize that they are the hidden fountainhead of knowledge development and therefore the key to the challenge of the knowledge economy. The third step is to appreciate the paradox that these informal structures require specific managerial efforts to develop them and to integrate them into the organization so that their full power can be leveraged.

Communities of practice are the new frontier. They may seem unfamiliar now, but in five to ten years they may be as common to discussions about organization as business units and teams are today—if managers learn how to make them a central part of their companies' success.

Communities in Action

COMMUNITIES OF PRACTICE add value to organizations in several important ways:

They help drive strategy

Communities of practice are the heart and soul of the World Bank's knowledge management strategy. Some communities of practice have existed for years at the bank, but they were mostly small and fragmented. That has changed now that the bank has made knowledge management the key to its goal of becoming the "knowledge bank"—providing high-quality information and know-how about economic development.

The bank's decision to fund communities of practice, for example, led to a significant increase in the number of organizationwide communities—it's now over 100—and in the intensity of participation. As the bank supplements its emphasis on lending money with providing development expertise, these communities will increasingly contribute to the bank's strategic direction.

They start new lines of business

Consider how a group of consultants from one firm created a community that eventually generated an entirely new line of business. The group met regularly at O'Hare airport between engagements with clients. Its domain was retail marketing in the banking industry, and the meetings focused on new business opportunities for clients. Over a two-year period, the initial group of five to seven consultants attracted many others within the firm. Four years after the first meeting, the community had created a new line of marketing approaches for financial services companies. And it convened 200 people from the firm in New Orleans for its annual conference. The community acted like a petri dish for entrepreneurial insights that ultimately generated more clients, shaped the firm's strategy, and enhanced its reputation.

They solve problems quickly

Members of a community of practice know whom to ask for help with a problem. They also know how to ask questions so that peers can quickly comprehend and focus on the heart of the problem. At Buckman Labs, members of communities of practice from around the world routinely respond to practice-specific queries within 24 hours. In one case, an employee trying to help a pulp mill customer in the Pacific Northwest solve a dye-retention problem received several responses within a day from expert peers in Europe, South Africa, and Canada—and one response provided exactly the solution the customer needed.

They transfer best practices

A community of practice does much more than work on specific problems. It's also an ideal forum for sharing and spreading best practices across a company.

Consider how the former Chrysler made this work, beginning in the early 1990s when the company broke up its functional departments to organize around car platforms such as small cars and minivans. Chrysler's leaders feared they would lose functional expertise and the ability to keep up with leading-edge change. To address those concerns, senior managers and engineers formed communities of practice known as "tech clubs," which were composed of experts from different car platforms. The clubs helped the company successfully make the move to platforms, a change that cut R&D costs and car-development cycle times by more than half.

Today the tech clubs are an important part of the integration of DaimlerChrysler. The clubs meet regularly to discuss questions in 11 areas of product development, including body design, electronics, and vehicle development. They analyze variations in practice and set standards. Engineers who participate in the clubs are responsible for developing and maintaining an Engineering Book of Knowledge, a database that captures information on compliance standards, supplier specifications, and best practices.

They develop professional skills

Studies have shown that apprentices learn as much from journeymen and more advanced apprentices as they do from master craftsmen. It seems clear, then, that effective learning depends on the availability of peers and their willingness to act as mentors and coaches. That applies not only to the education of inexperienced workers but also to that of experts. The best neurosurgeons don't rely simply on their own brilliance; they read peer-reviewed journals, attend conferences in which their colleagues discuss new research, and travel great distances to work alongside surgeons who are developing innovative techniques.

Some companies have found that communities of practice are particularly effective arenas for fostering professional development. At IBM, communities of practice hold their own conferences, both in person and online. Presentations, hallway conversations, dinners, and chat rooms are opportunities for members to exchange ideas, build skills, and develop networks.

They help companies recruit and retain talent

American Management Systems has found that communities of practice help the company win the war (or at least some of the battles) for talent. Thus a consultant who was planning to leave the company decided to stay after peers at a community forum found project opportunities for her that were tailor-made to her interests and expertise. Other valuable consultants—at least six, by one manager's count—stayed with the company after being invited to join a prestigious community of practice that would enable them to develop skills and find new clients.

Originally published in January 2000
Reprint R00110

How the Right Measures Help Teams Excel

CHRISTOPHER MEYER

Executive Summary

AT MANY COMPANIES THAT HAVE moved from control-oriented, functional hierarchies to faster and flatter multifunctional teams, traditional performance-measurement systems not only fail to support these teams but also undermine them, Christopher Meyer argues. Many managers fail to realize that traditional measures, which focus on results, may help them keep score on the performance of their businesses but do not help a multifunctional team monitor the activities or capabilities that enable it to perform a given process. Nor do such *results measures* tell team members what they must do to improve their performance.

How should performance-measurement systems be overhauled to maximize the effectiveness of teams? First, the overarching purpose of the system should be to help a team, rather than top managers, gauge its progress.

Next, a truly empowered team must play the lead role in designing its own measurement system. And because a team is responsible for a value-delivery process that cuts across several functions, it must create new measures to track this process. Finally, a team should adopt only a handful of measures.

Senior managers play an important role in helping teams develop performance measures by dictating strategic goals, ensuring that each team understands how it fits into those goals, and training a team to devise its own measures But managers must never make the mistake of thinking that they know what is best for the team. If they do, they will have returned to the command-and-control days of yore, and they will have rendered their empowered teams powerless.

MANY EXECUTIVES HAVE realized that process-focused, multifunctional teams can dramatically improve the way their companies deliver products and services to customers. Most executives have not yet realized, however, that such teams need new performance-measurement systems to fulfill their promise.

The design of any performance-measurement system should reflect the basic operating assumptions of the organization it supports. If the organization changes and the measurement system doesn't, the latter will be at best ineffective or, more likely, counterproductive. At many companies that have moved from control-oriented, functional hierarchies to a faster and flatter team-based approach, traditional performance-measurement systems not only fail to support the new teams but also undermine them. Indeed, traditional systems often heighten the conflicts between multifunctional teams and functions that are vexing many organizations today.

Ideally, a measurement system designed to support a team-based organization should help teams overcome two major obstacles to their effectiveness: getting functions to provide expertise to teams when they need it and getting people from different functions on a team to speak a common language. Traditional measurement systems don't solve those problems.

The primary role of traditional measurement systems, which are still used in most companies, is to pull "good information" up so that senior managers can make "good decisions" that flow down. To that end, each relatively independent function has its own set of measures, whose main purpose is to inform top managers about its activities. Marketing tracks market share, operations watches inventory, finance monitors costs, and so on.

Such *results measures* tell an organization where it stands in its effort to achieve goals but not how it got there or, even more important, what it should do differently. Most results measures track what goes on within a function, not what happens across functions. The few cross-functional results measures in organizations are typically financial, like revenues, gross margins, costs of goods sold, capital assets, and debt, and they exist only to help top managers. In contrast, *process measures* monitor the tasks and activities throughout an organization that produce a given result. Such measures are essential for cross-functional teams that are responsible for processes that deliver an entire service or product to customers, like order fulfillment or new-product development. Unlike a traditional, functional organization, a team-based organization not only makes it possible to use process measures but also requires them.

How should performance-measurement systems be overhauled to maximize the effectiveness of teams? Here are four guiding principles:

1. **The overarching purpose of a measurement system should be to help a team, rather than top managers, gauge its progress.** A team's measurement system should primarily be a tool for telling the team when it must take corrective action. The measurement system must also provide top managers with a means to intervene if the team runs into problems it cannot solve by itself. But even if a team has good measures, they will be of little use if senior managers use them to control the team. A measurement system is not only the measures but also the way they are used.

2. **A truly empowered team must play the lead role in designing its own measurement system.** A team will know best what sort of measurement system it needs, but the team should not design this system in isolation. Senior managers must ensure that the resulting measurement system is consistent with the company's strategy.

3. **Because a team is responsible for a value-delivery process that cuts across several functions (like product development, order fulfillment, or customer service), it must create measures to track that process.** In a traditional functional organization, no single function is responsible for a total value-delivery process; thus there are no good ways

to measure those processes. In contrast, the purpose of the multifunctional team approach is to create a structure—the team—that is responsible for a complete value-delivery process. Teams must create measures that support their mission, or they will not fully exploit their ability to perform the process faster and in a way that is more responsive to customer demands.

A process measure that a product-development team might use is one that tracks staffing levels to make sure that the necessary people are on a given team at the right time. Another measure is the number or percentage of new or unique parts to be used in a product. While such parts may offer a performance advantage, the more a product contains, the greater the likelihood that there will be difficult design, integration, inventory, manufacturing, and assembly issues.

Having sung the praises of process measures, let me throw in a qualification: while such measures are extremely important, teams still need to use some traditional measures, like one that tracks receivables, to ensure that functional and team results are achieved. Functional excellence is a prerequisite for team excellence.

4. **A team should adopt only a handful of measures.** The long-held view that "what gets measured gets done" has spurred managers to react to intensifying competition by piling more and more measures on their operations in a bid to encourage employees to work harder. As a result, team members end up spending too much time collecting data and

monitoring their activities and not enough time managing the project. I have seen dozens of teams spend too much time at meetings discussing the mechanics of the measurement system instead of discussing what to *do*. As a general rule, if a team has more than 15 measures, it should take a fresh look at the importance of each one.

Trying to run a team without a good, simple guidance system is like trying to drive a car without a dashboard. We might do it in a pinch but not as a matter of practice, because we'd lack the necessary information—the speed, the amount of fuel, the engine temperature—to ensure that we reach our destination. Companies may find it helpful to create a computerized "dashboard," which inexpensive graphics software has made easy to do. (See "The Team Dashboard" at the end of this article.)

The lack of an effective measurement system, or dashboard, can even prevent teams from making it much past the starting line. After companies first adopt the team approach, teams must typically prove to skeptical senior and middle managers that the power these managers have wielded can be handed to the teams without the business spinning out of control. A team can offer no such proof if it lacks the tools to track its performance.

What operations executive, for example, would be willing to let a new-product development team manage the transition from an existing product to a new one if the team did not have a measure that tracked old product inventory from the factory throughout the distribution channel? Without such information, the company might end up stuck with lots of an unsellable old product. And what development executive would be willing to hand over responsibility for a project if he or she did not see that the product-development team was able to track cost, quality, and schedule?

Many managers fail to realize that results measures like profits, market share, and cost, which may help them keep score on the performance of their businesses, do not help a multifunctional team, or any organization, monitor the activities or capabilities that enable it to perform a given process. Nor do such measures tell team members what they must do to improve their performance.

An 8% drop in quarterly profits accompanied by a 10% rise in service costs, for example, does not tell a customer-service team what its service technicians should do differently on their next call. Process measures, however, examine the actions and capabilities that contributed to the situation. Knowing that the average time spent per service call rose 15% last month and that, as a result, the number of late calls rose 10% would explain to the technicians why service costs had gone up and customer satisfaction and profits had gone down.

The most commonly used results measures in product development are schedule and cost. But the fact that a program is six months late and $2 million over budget doesn't tell anyone what went wrong or what to do differently. In contrast, tracking staffing levels during the course of a project—a process measure that might include not only the number of bodies but also the years of experience in major job categories—can radically affect a team's performance. Many product-development teams, for example, do a poor job planning exactly when they will need people with a certain functional expertise. Not having all the necessary people at a particular stage often leads to expensive and time-consuming efforts to fix problems that the right people would have detected earlier.

This is exactly what I saw happen at a company that had given a multifunctional team seven months to develop a consumer product for testing blood-sugar levels. The team began work on July 1 and had a February 1 target date for launching the product. Although the company had named the people from the critical functions who would serve on the team well before the effort got under way, Mary, the manufacturing representative, did not join the team until mid-August. By then, people from marketing and development engineering had already made some best-guess decisions about significant packaging and manufacturing issues. After one week on the team, Mary raised serious questions about many of those decisions, and the team decided to adopt her suggestions and retrace its steps. Not only was Mary's arrival on the team very awkward, but also the program slipped by three weeks within the first two months.

A team's reliance on traditional measures can also cause its members to forget the team's goal and revert to their old functional way of working—or fighting—with one another. Consider the case of Ford Motor Company during the development of a luxury model in 1991. The project was one of Ford's first attempts to use multifunctional teams for product development. By and large, the team's measurement system was a collection of the individual measures that each function on the team (styling, body engineering, power train, purchasing, finance, etc.) had used for years.

Shortly before team members were to sign off on the car's design and begin engineering the body, a controversy developed over the door handle, which was different from the ones Ford had been using. One reason for the controversy was that each function made different assumptions about the relative importance of the factors contributing to the product's costs and competitiveness.

Members from the purchasing and finance departments feared that the handle would be too expensive. Their gauges were the cost of manufacturing the handle and its warranty costs. The people from design and body engineering responded that the handle's design was no more complex than that of existing handles. And because there was no basis for assuming that its warranty costs would be higher, they argued, the cost of manufacturing the handle should be the main issue in the cost debate. They submitted a bid from a vendor on Ford's approved vendor list as proof that the handle would be no more expensive to make. In addition, they argued, purchasing and finance were not giving enough weight to the importance of the handle's design in the overall design of the car.

The purchasing representative was still not satisfied about the warranty costs. He said that handles made by other approved vendors had had lower warranty costs than handles made by the vendor whose bid had been submitted. After a short shouting match, the design and engineering people gave up.

During the debate, no one asked the critical question: Would the new handle increase the car's ability to compete in the marketplace? Since the model's distinctive styling was a critical competitive element, the new handle might have helped the vehicle capture enough additional customers to more than compensate for higher warranty costs. Adopting the old handle was not necessarily the best decision, and this last-minute design change, which in turn required other changes, added at least one week to the development process. The members of this product-development team were still thinking as they did in their functions, where nobody had an overview of what would make the product succeed in the marketplace.

What kind of measures could have helped the team avoid its win-lose battle over cost versus style? One possibility would have been a measure that incorporated several product attributes, such as product cost, features, service, and packaging, to enable the team to assess trade-offs. This may have helped the team realize that an undetermined factor—the proposed handle's warranty costs—should not have influenced the decision so heavily.

W HEN CROSS-FUNCTIONAL TEAMS are being established, many companies do not institute a measurement system that supports the company's strategy, ensures senior managers that there won't be unpleasant surprises, and, last but not least, truly empowers the teams. Let me offer a generic process that most companies can implement. I'll start with the role of top managers.

In two articles on the *balanced scorecard* ("The Balanced Scorecard—Measures That Drive Performance," HBR January–February 1992, and "Putting the Balanced Scorecard to Work," HBR September–October 1993), Robert S. Kaplan and David P. Norton provide managers with a valuable framework for integrating a company's strategic objectives and competitive demands into its performance-measurement system. They urge managers to augment their traditional financial measures with measures of customer satisfaction, internal processes, and innovation and improvement activities.

What Kaplan and Norton do not explain is how such an approach can be applied to team-based organizations. I believe that it can, with one caveat: senior managers should create the strategic context for the teams but not the measures. Senior managers should dictate strategic goals, ensure that each team understands how its job fits into the strategy, and provide training so that the team can devise its own measures. But to ensure that owner-ship of and accountability for performance remains with the teams, managers must require the teams to decide which measures will best help them perform their jobs.

For example, the managers of a multinational com-puter company established an ambitious strategic goal for all of the company's product-development teams to reduce their cycle times by more than 50% within three years. But rather than dictating how the teams measure cycle time, managers asked each team to select its own measures. To help the teams in this effort, managers pro-vided training in cycle-time reduction and a very broad selection of measures from which the teams could choose.

Top managers and a team should jointly establish rules about when or under what circumstances man-agers will review the team's performance and its mea-surement system. A team should know at the outset that it will have to review the measures it has selected with top managers to ensure that they are consistent with corporate strategy and that it may have to adjust its measures. The team should also promise to renegotiate with managers any major changes in the measures made during the course of the project. As I will discuss later, measures should not be carved in stone.

The team and senior managers should also set boundaries, which, if crossed, will signal that the team has run into trouble serious enough to trigger an "out-of-bounds" management review. Such an approach keeps managers informed without disenfranchising the team.

During an out-of-bounds review, teams and managers must define the problem and decide what corrective action to take. The team must retain responsibility for calling and running the review and executing any decisions. It must be clear that the purpose of the reviews is for senior managers to help the teams solve problems, not to find fault.

Some product-development teams actually negotiate written contracts with senior managers at the start of a project. The contracts define the product, including features and quality targets; the targeted cost to the customer; the program cost; financial information like revenues, gross margins, and cost of goods sold; and the schedule. During the contract negotiations, management ensures that the overall program, including the measures, supports the company's strategy.

The contract also establishes rules for management reviews. For example, one company requires only two planned reviews. The first comes at the end of the design phase so that management can confirm that the product still meets the market need before the company invests in expensive tooling. The second review is after production is under way so that management can learn about and pass on to other teams any advances that the team has made, like designing a particular component to be manufactured easily, and can solve unforeseen production problems early on. During the entire design phase, the team is free to proceed without any contact with management unless it has broken or knows it will break its commitments on product features, performance, product and development costs, or schedule.

The main problem at most companies that now use multifunctional teams is that top managers use a team's measurement system to monitor and control projects or processes. Even if unintentional, such behavior will inevitably undermine the effectiveness of any team.

This is what happened when a Ford manufacturing plant turned to multifunctional teams to improve product quality but didn't change management's command-and-control mind-set.

The company grouped line workers from various functional areas into teams and trained them to collect and analyze data so that they could resolve quality problems on their own. But then came the mistake: the division managers asked quality engineers, who supposedly had been sent to assist the teams, to send a monthly report on the plant's quality and plans for improving it. In turn, the quality engineers asked the teams for their data.

Over time, the teams began to depend on the quality engineers to analyze the data and waited for the engineers' directions before taking action. The engineers recognized what was happening but felt caught in a bind because the division managers wanted them, rather than the teams, to provide the reports. Problems that the teams had been able to resolve on their own in a day or two began to require the involvement of the quality engineers and twice the time. And the quality engineers asked for more engineers to help them support the teams.

The division managers became very frustrated. Given all their verbal support for empowering teams, they couldn't understand why the teams didn't act empowered.

Wʜᴇɴ ᴀ ɢʀᴏᴜᴘ ᴏꜰ ᴘᴇᴏᴘʟᴇ builds a measurement system, it also builds a team. One benefit of having a team create its own measurement system is that members who hail from different functions end up creating a common language, which they need in order to work as an effective team. Until a group creates a common language, it can't reach a common definition of goals or problems. Instead of acting like a team, the group will act like a collection of functions.

As a first step, the team should develop a work plan that can serve as a process map of the critical tasks and capabilities required to complete the project. The second step is to make sure that everyone understands the team's goals in the same way. Team members frequently start out believing that they share an understanding of their goals only to discover when they begin developing performance measures how wrong they were.

After the goals have been confirmed, the appropriate team members should develop individual measures for gauging the team's progress in achieving a given goal and identifying the conditions that would trigger an out-of-bounds review. In addition, each member should come to the next meeting with two or three gauges that he or she considers most effective for monitoring his or her functional area. In an attempt to push team members to focus on overall goals and the total value-delivery process as they develop measures, they should be encouraged to include process measures. (See "Creating Process Measures" at the end of this article.)

At the next meeting, each member should explain what his or her proposed measures track and why they are important. Everyone should make an effort to define any terms or concepts that are unfamiliar to others. One important rule is that no question is a "dumb question."

So-called dumb questions are often the most valuable because they test the potential value of each measure in the most obvious terms.

Some measures will be either eliminated or agreed on very quickly. The hard work will be assessing those that fall in between. No final decisions should be made until all the gauges accepted or still in contention are tested as a unit against the following criteria:

- Are critical team objectives (like filling an order within 24 hours) tracked?

- Are all out-of-bounds conditions monitored?

- Are the critical variables required to reach the goal (like having enough skilled personnel to run an order-entry system) tracked?

- Would management approve the system as is or seek changes?

- Is there any gauge that wouldn't cause the team to change its behavior if the needle swung from one side to another? If so, eliminate it.

- Are there too many gauges? As I mentioned earlier, if a team has more than 15 measures, it should take a second look at each one.

After a team's measures have passed this test, the system is ready for the management review.

A TEAM CAN PRESERVE the value of its performance-measurement system by diligently adding and eliminating gauges, as required, during the project or task.

Measures that were relevant during the early stages in the development of a new product will undoubtedly become irrelevant as the product nears production. In most cases, teams realize that and plan for changes during the development of their measurement systems. But priorities often change during a project, which means that measures should be changed too. And sometimes measures prove not to be so useful after all and should be dropped. A team should also regularly audit the data being fed into its measurement system to make sure they are accurate and timely.

Managers are still in the early stages of learning how to maximize the effectiveness of multifunctional teams that are incorporated into their functional organizations. The same applies to the measurement systems used to guide both. As companies gain experience, they will discover that some specific measures can be used over and over again by different teams undertaking similar tasks or projects. But managers should be on their guard lest they do with performance-measurement systems what they have done with so many management tools: assume that one size fits all. Managers can systematize the process that teams use to create their measurement systems. They can also catalog the measures that appear to have been most effective in particular applications. But managers must never make the mistake of thinking that they know what is best for the team. If they do, they will have crossed the line and returned to the command-and-control ways of yore. And they will have rendered their empowered teams powerless.

The Team Dashboard

SPREADSHEETS ARE THE MOST common format companies use to display their performance measures. But if a measurement system should function like a car's dashboard by providing a multifunctional team with the information it needs to complete its journey, why not actually construct a dashboard? The dashboard format, complete with colorful graphic indicators and other easy-to-read gauges, makes it much easier for a team to monitor its progress and know when it must change direction. A multifunctional team called Lethal, which designed and built a 2.5-inch disk drive for the Quantum Corporation in Milpitas, California, used the displayed dashboard.

Quantum had begun using multifunctional development teams only nine months before it established the Lethal team late in 1989. Lethal's core group included representatives from marketing, manufacturing, engineering, quality assurance, finance, and human resources. While Quantum was a strong player in the 3.5-inch drive segment, it had never made 2.5-inch drives. On top of this technical challenge, managers wanted Lethal to deliver the drive in 14 months—10 months less than similar projects had taken.

Larry, the team's principal leader, who came from engineering, was very skeptical about whether or not Quantum's past development practices would enable Lethal to reach its 14-month goal. When he asked leaders from previous teams what they would do differently, all said they would try to find a better way to detect problems early. The teams would gather all the right players, but too many problems still ended up being resolved in the functions. Larry recognized one reason for that situation: the teams had used measurement systems designed for hierarchical, functional organizations. He thought Lethal could do better.

When the team began trying to establish a schedule, its members quickly discovered that development engineering was the only function that had provided a

Lethal's Dashboard

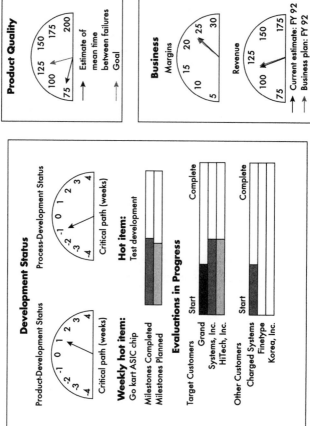

Product Quality

Estimate of mean time between failures
Goal

Business

Margins

Revenue

↑ Current estimate: FY 92
↑ Business plan: FY 92

Development Status

Product-Development Status

Critical path (weeks)

Weekly hot item:
Go kart ASIC chip

Milestones Completed
Milestones Planned

Process-Development Status

Critical path (weeks)

Hot item:
Test development

Evaluations in Progress

Target Customers
Grand Systems, Inc.
HiTech, Inc.

Start   Complete

Other Customers
Charged Systems
FineType
Korea, Inc.

Start   Complete

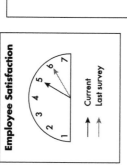

Employee Satisfaction

↑ Current
↑ Last survey

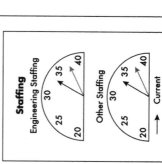

Staffing

Engineering Staffing

Other Staffing

↑ Current
↑ Goal

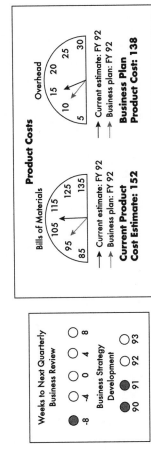

Product Costs

Bills of Materials

85 — 95 — 105 — 115 — 125 — 135

→ Current estimate: FY 92
⇢ Business plan: FY 92

**Current Product
Cost Estimate: 152**

Overhead

5 — 10 — 15 — 20 — 25 — 30

→ Current estimate: FY 92
⇢ Business plan: FY 92

**Business Plan
Product Cost: 138**

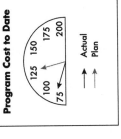

Program Cost to Date

75 — 100 — 125 — 150 — 175 — 200

→ Actual
⇢ Plan

Weeks to Next Quarterly
Business Review

-8   -4   0   4   8

Business Strategy
Development

90   91   92   93

complete schedule for performing its tasks. The others had only sketched out major milestones. In addition, individual team members were often unsure what the others' schedules meant, and none of the schedules had been integrated. Marketing had even gone ahead and set a date for the product launch without consulting development engineering!

After this revelation, the team members decided to spell out the details of all the functional schedules in terms that everyone could understand. They then integrated those schedules into one master product-development schedule, which product-development programs often lack.

In addition to this schedule monitor and a milestone gauge, the dashboard contains a variety of other results measures, which development teams typically use to track their progress in achieving the key strategic goals that will determine whether or not top managers consider the project a success. Lethal's goals included creating a product that could be manufactured at a targeted cost (tracked by the "Overhead" and "Bills of Materials" gauges) and had a competitive quality level (tracked by the "Product Quality" gauge). The dashboard also has results measures for tracking the product's success in achieving profit margin and revenue targets once it is on the market. But such results measures tell a team only where it stands, not why it stands there. To do the latter, Lethal adopted the first process measures used by multifunctional teams in the company.

Previous teams at Quantum had focused on developing the product and treated as secondary such tasks as developing the methods and equipment for testing. Only after teams discovered that early prototypes couldn't be adequately tested did those issues receive attention. To avoid such a bottleneck, Lethal adopted a separate process-development gauge for all the tasks involved in manufacturing, including testing.

A similar discussion resulted in a decision to include staffing gauges on the dashboard. People for areas like testing, manufacturing, and marketing had to be hired early enough so that they would be on board when the team needed them. If the team waited until the development of testing methods and equipment were supposed to start before hiring test engineers, the schedule could slip by at least six weeks.

Larry's motive for suggesting the employee-satisfaction gauge was simple: unhappy team members won't keep to an ambitious schedule. The position of the "Current" needle reflects the team leaders' opinion of the team's morale. The position of the "Last survey" needle reflects the most recent survey of all team members. By forcing themselves to monitor morale, the leaders discovered that people were concerned about such things as the shortage of lab space and access to the workstations and were able to do something about those issues before they hurt morale.

The indicator lights in the lower left-hand corner of the dashboard were designed to ensure that the team allocated enough time to planning. While weekly team meetings were adequate for dealing with many issues, some, like product-launch planning, required more preparation. Because of the program's intensity, team members worried that issues that couldn't be solved quickly would eventually cause a bottleneck. Scheduling a half- or full-day meeting that everyone could attend would often take at least four weeks. John from marketing suggested that the team use the indicator lights as a reminder to schedule time for planning sessions.

The team quickly realized which gauges were not useful. John from finance argued that determining Lethal's expenses for the "Program Cost to Date" gauge was nearly impossible since the company did not have a project-based accounting system. More-over, top managers rarely asked about an individual program's costs because they hardly varied from project to project. Since nobody on the team changed his or her behavior if the program-cost gauge dropped or increased, the team decided to eliminate it.

The team succeeded in getting potential customers for the 2.5-inch disk drive to approve the company as a qualified supplier in 16 months—2 months over the original target date but still 33% faster than previous teams. However, the drive took longer to move through the actual qualification phase than previous drives. The "Evaluations in Progress" gauges helped Lethal track its progress with potential customers but did not help the team discover a key problem until relatively late: Lethal's test procedures were more rigorous than those used by potential customers, which made it look as if the drives' failure rate was relatively high. On the basis of these data, potential customers would not qualify the company as a supplier.

Could a dashboard with different gauges have detected the problem early enough to solve it? Probably not. Like any performance-measurement tool, the dashboard is not a replacement for the decision maker.

Creating Process Measures

THERE ARE FOUR BASIC STEPS to creating process measures: defining what kinds of factors, such as time,

cost, quality, and product performance, are critical to sat-
isfying customers; mapping the cross-functional process
used to deliver results; identifying the critical tasks and
capabilities required to complete the process successfully; and, finally, designing measures that track those
tasks and capabilities. The most effective process measures are often those that express relative terms. For
example, a measure that tracks the percentage of new
or unique parts is usually more valuable than one that
tracks the absolute number.

Here's how the parts and service operation of a
Europe-based car company created process measures.

The warehousing function had traditionally measured
its performance by tracking how often parts ordered by
dealers could be filled immediately from the warehouse
shelf. If a stock picker found a gasket on the warehouse
shelf—meaning that it did not have to be ordered—that
counted as a "first fill."

When the organization began using teams, it put the
warehousing and the dealer-service groups on a multifunctional team charged with improving the total service
process, from product breakdown through repair. The
team reexamined the current performance measures and
concluded that, from the dealer's perspective, the first-fill
measure was meaningless. Dealers—and the final customers—didn't care where the part came from; they just
wanted to know when they'd receive it. And just
because a part was on the warehouse shelf did not
ensure that it would get to a dealer quickly; the sloppy
handling of orders and shipping problems could also
cause delays.

Because the new team was responsible for the entire
process, it mapped all the steps in the service cycle, from
the moment the warehouse received a dealer's order to
the moment the dealer received the part, and the time

each step took. The team then identified its critical tasks and capabilities, which included the order-entry operation, the management-information system for tracking orders and inventories, warehouse operations, and shipping. The team created cycle-time measures for six to eight sub-processes, which helped the team see how much time was being spent on each step of the process relative to the value of that process. With this information, the team could begin figuring out how to reduce cycle time without sacrificing quality. The resulting changes included reducing the copies made of each order and the number of signatures required to authorize filling it. Within six months, the team was able to reduce the service cycle considerably. Not coincidentally, dealer complaints fell by a comparable amount.

Originally published in May–June 1994
Reprint 94305

Author's note: The author would like to thank Steven C. Wheelwright, who provided valuable guidance for this article.

The Nut Island Effect

When Good Teams Go Wrong

PAUL F. LEVY

Executive Summary

THE TEAM THAT OPERATED the Nut Island sewage treatment plant in Quincy, Massachusetts, was every manager's dream. Members of the group performed difficult, dangerous work without complaint. They needed little supervision. They improvised their way around operational difficulties and budgetary constraints. They were dedicated to the organization's mission.

But their hard work let to catastrophic failure. How could such a good team go so wrong? In this article, the author tells the story of the Nut Island plant and identifies a common, yet destructive organizational dynamic that can strike any business.

The Nut Island effect begins with a deeply committed team that is isolated from a company's mainstream activities. Pitted against this team is its senior management. Preoccupied with high-visibility problems, management assigns the team a vital but behind-the-scenes task. Allowed considerable autonomy, team members become adept at managing themselves. Management takes the team's self-sufficiency for granted and ignores team members when they ask for help. When trouble strikes and management is unresponsive, team members feel betrayed and develop an us-against-the-world mentality. They stay out of management's line of sight, hiding problems. The team begins to make up its own rules, which mask grave problems in its operations. Management, disinclined in the first place to focus on the team's work, is easily misled by team members' skillful disguising of its performance deficiencies. The resulting stalemate typically can be broken only by an external event.

The Nut Island story serves as a warning to managers who concentrate their efforts on their organization's most visible shortcomings: sometimes the most debilitating problems are the ones we can't see.

They were every manager's dream team. They performed difficult, dirty, dangerous work without complaint, they put in thousands of hours of unpaid overtime, and they even dipped into their own pockets to buy spare parts. They needed virtually no supervision, handled their own staffing decisions, cross-trained each other, and ingeniously improvised their way around operational difficulties and budgetary constraints. They had tremendous esprit de corps and a deep commitment to the organization's mission.

There was just one problem: their hard work helped lead to that mission's catastrophic failure.

The team that traced this arc of futility were the 80 or
so men and women who operated the Nut Island sewage
treatment plant in Quincy, Massachusetts, from the late
1960s until it was decommissioned in 1997. During that
period, these exemplary workers were determined to
protect Boston Harbor from pollution. Yet in one six-
month period in 1982, in the ordinary course of business,
they released 3.7 billion gallons of raw sewage into the
harbor. Other routine procedures they performed to keep
the harbor clean, such as dumping massive amounts of
chlorine into otherwise untreated sewage, actually wors-
ened the harbor's already dreadful water quality.

How could such a good team go so wrong? And why
were the people of the Nut Island plant—not to mention
their supervisors in Boston—unable to recognize that
they were sabotaging themselves and their mission?
These questions go to the heart of what I call *the Nut
Island effect*, a destructive organizational dynamic I
came to understand after serving four and a half years as
the executive director of the public authority responsible
for the metropolitan Boston sewer system.

Since leaving that job, I have shared the Nut Island
story with managers from a wide range of organizations.
Quite a few of them—hospital administrators, research
librarians, senior corporate officers—react with a shock
of recognition. They, too, have seen the Nut Island effect
in action where they work.

Comparing notes with these managers, I have found
that each instance of the Nut Island effect features a similar set of antagonists—a dedicated, cohesive team and
distracted senior managers—whose conflict follows a
predictable behavioral pattern through five stages. (The
path of the Nut Island effect is illustrated in "Five Steps to

Failure" at the end of this article.) The sequence of the
stages may vary somewhat from case to case, but in its
broad outlines, the syndrome is unchanging. In a dynamic
that is not so much a vicious circle as a vicious spiral, the
relationship between the two sides gradually crumbles
under the weight of mutual mistrust and incomprehen-
sion until it can hardly be called a relationship at all.

The consequences of this organizational pathology
are not always as vivid and unmistakable as they were in
the case of the Nut Island team. More frequently, I sus-
pect, its effects are like a slow leak—subtle, gradual, and
difficult to trace. Nevertheless, the Nut Island story
should serve as a warning to managers who spend the
bulk of their time on an organization's most visible and
obvious shortcomings: sometimes the most debilitating
problems are the ones we can't see.

The Nut Island Effect Defined

The Nut Island effect begins with a homogeneous, deeply
committed team working in isolation that can be physical, psychological, or both. Pitted against this team are
its senior supervisors, who are usually separated from
the team by several layers of management. In the first
stage of the Nut Island effect, senior management, preoccupied with high-visibility problems, assigns the team a
vital but behind-the-scenes task. This is a crucial feature:
the team carries out its task far from the eye of the public
or customers. Allowed a great deal of autonomy, team
members become adept at organizing and managing
themselves, and the unit develops a proud and distinct
identity. In the second stage, senior management begins
to take the team's self-sufficiency for granted and ignores
team members when they ask for help or try to warn of

impending trouble. Management's apparent indifference breeds resentment in the team members, reinforces its isolation, and heightens its sense of itself as a band of heroic outcasts. In the third stage, an us-against-the-world mentality takes hold among team members. They make it a priority to stay out of management's line of sight, which leads them to deny or minimize problems and avoid asking for help.

This isolation leads to the fourth stage of the conflict. With no external input on practices and operating guidelines, the team begins to make up its own rules. The team tells itself that the rules enable it to fulfill its mission. In fact, these rules mask the deterioration of the team's working environment and deficiencies in the team's performance. In the fifth stage, both the team and senior management form distorted pictures of reality that are very difficult to correct. Team members come to believe they are the only ones who really understand their work. They close their ears when well-meaning outsiders attempt to point out problems. Management tells itself that no news is good news and continues to ignore the team and its task. Only some kind of external event can break this stalemate. Perhaps management disbands the team or pulls the plug on its project. Perhaps a crisis forces the team to ask for help and snaps management out of its complacency. Even then, team members may not understand the extent of their difficulties or recognize that their efforts may have aggravated the very problems they were attempting to solve. Management, for its part, may be unable to recognize the role it played in setting in motion this self-reinforcing spiral of failure.

That, then, is an outline of the Nut Island effect. Here is how it played out at a small sewage treatment plant on the edge of Boston Harbor.

The Nut Island Story

Nut Island is actually a small peninsula in Quincy, Massachusetts, a mostly blue-collar city of 85,000 located about ten miles south of Boston. Sitting at the southern entrance to Boston Harbor, Nut Island was a favorite landmark for seventeenth-century sailors, who savored the scent of what one early European settler called the "divers arematicall herbes, and plants" that grew there. "Shipps have come from Virginea where there have bin scarce five men able to hale a rope," the settler wrote, "untill they come [near Nut Island], and smell the sweet aire of the shore, where they have suddainly recovered."

By 1952, when the Nut Island treatment plant went into operation, the herbs and sweet air were long gone. Before the plant came on line, raw sewage from much of Boston and the surrounding area was piped straight into the harbor, fouling local beaches and fisheries and posing a serious health hazard to the surrounding community.

The Nut Island plant was billed as the solution to Quincy's wastewater problem. Hailed in the local press for its "modern design," it was supposed to treat all the sewage produced in the southern half of the Boston metropolitan area, then release it about a mile out into the harbor. From the first, though, the plant's suitability for the task was questionable. The facility was designed to handle sewage inflows of up to 285 million gallons per day, comfortably above the 112 million gallons that flowed in on an average day. But high tides and heavy rains could increase the flow to three times the daily average, straining the plant to its limits and compromising its performance.

During most of the 30 years covered in this article, the team charged with running the plant was headed by superintendent Bill Smith, operations chief Jack Madden, and laboratory head Frank Mac Kinnon. The three joined me recently for a reunion at Nut Island, which has been converted to a headworks that collects sewage from the southern Boston region and delivers it north through a tunnel under Boston Harbor to the city's vast new treatment plant on Deer Island. The men's affection for each other is evident, as are the lingering remnants of plant hierarchy. When someone has to speak for the entire group, Mac Kinnon and Madden still defer to Smith.

The three friends don't need much prompting to launch into reminiscences of their years at Nut Island, which they still view as the happiest time of their working lives. They laugh often as they tell stories about the old days, featuring characters with nicknames like Sludgie and Twinkie, and they seem cheerfully oblivious to the hair-raising conditions that were part of daily life at the plant. When Smith talks about once finding himself neck-deep in wastewater as he worked in the pump room, he speaks without a hint of horror or disgust. It's just a good story. "It was fun," Smith says, and his two friends nod in agreement. Holding an old sewer plant together with chewing gum and baling wire really is their idea of a good time.

Throughout our talk, the men frequently refer to themselves and their coworkers as a family. But Nut Island had not always been such a harmonious place. When Smith arrived there in 1963, fresh out of the navy, he walked into a three-way cold war among operations, maintenance, and the plant's laboratory. Each side viewed its own function as essential and looked down on the other groups' workers as incompetents. "The maintenance guys thought the lab guys were a bunch of college boys," says Smith, a short, powerfully built man who at age 63 still has more black than gray in his long, pony-tailed hair and thick beard. "And the guys in the lab said the maintenance guys were just grease monkeys."

For the next few years, Smith did what he could to "get a little cooperation going." By 1968, he had gained Madden and Mac Kinnon as allies. Before long, they had weeded out most of the plant's shirkers and complainers and assembled a cohesive team. The people they hired were much like themselves: hardworking, grateful for the security of a public sector job, and happy to stay out of the spotlight. Many were veterans of World War II or the Korean War, accustomed to managing frequent crises in harsh working conditions—just what awaited them at the aging, undersized, underfunded plant. Tony Kucikas was typical of the breed. He signed on in 1968 after being discharged from the navy, where he had worked as an engineer and machinist. When he walked into the plant on his first day, even the smell of oil was familiar, he recalls. "It reminded me so much of the engine room," he says, smiling at the memory. "I can remember walking down those first stairs and saying to myself, 'I'm going to like this,' because I felt right at home."

Nut Island's hiring practices helped create a tight-knit group, bonded by a common cause and shared values, but they also eliminated any "squeaky wheels" who might have questioned the team's standard operating procedures or alerted senior management to the plant's deteriorating condition. That was fine with Smith and his colleagues. Assembling a like-minded group made it easier for them to break down interdepartmental ani-mosities by cross-training plant personnel. The team leaders also made job satisfaction a priority, shifting peo-ple out of the jobs they were hired to do and into work that suited them better. These moves raised morale and created a strong sense of trust and ownership among plant workers.

Just how strong the sense of ownership was can be seen in the sacrifices the team made. Few people on Nut Island made more than $20,000 a year, low wages even in the 1960s and 1970s. Yet when there was no money for spare parts, team members would pitch in to buy the needed equipment. They were equally generous with their time. A sizable cadre of plant workers regularly put in far more than the requisite eight hours daily, but they only occasionally filed for overtime pay. In fact, several of the Nut Island alumni I interviewed seemed almost embarrassed when the subject came up, as if there was something slightly shameful about claiming the extra time.

From 1952 until 1985, the Nut Island plant fell under the purview of the Metropolitan District Commission (MDC), a regional infrastructure agency responsible for Greater Boston's parks and recreation areas, some of its major roads, and its water supplies and sewers. (In 1985, the Massachusetts state legislature, under pressure from a federal lawsuit, shifted responsibility for water and sewers to a new entity, the Massachusetts Water Resources Authority.) Throughout the early and mid-1900s, the MDC had been known for the quality of its engineers and the rigor of its management. It had constructed and operated water and sewer systems that were often cited as engineering marvels. By the 1960s, though, the MDC had become the plaything of the state legislature, whose members used the agency as a patronage mill. Commissioners rarely stayed more than two years, and their priorities reflected those of the legislators who controlled the MDC budget. The lawmakers understood full well that there were more votes to be gained by building skating rinks and swimming pools in their districts than by tuning up the sewer system, and they directed their funding and political pressure accordingly. As a result, control of Greater Boston's sewer system fell into the hands of political functionaries whose primary concern was to please their patrons in the statehouse. If that meant building another skating rink instead of maintaining Nut Island, so be it.

The attitude of the MDC's leadership toward the sewer division can be gauged by a story that became a staple of plant lore. As it was passed around, the story took on mythic power. It became a central component of the Nut Island team's self-definition.

It seems that one day, James W. Connell, Nut Island superintendent in the 1960s, went to Boston to ask the MDC commissioner for funds to perform long-deferred maintenance on essential equipment. The commissioner's only response: "Get rid of the dandelions."

Startled, the superintendent asked the commissioner to repeat himself.

"You heard me. I want you guys to take some money and get the dandelions off the lawn. The place looks terrible."

The story speaks for itself, but I would point out that it was something of a miracle that the commissioner had even laid eyes on the lawn and its dandelions. Visits to Nut Island by the MDC's upper management were so rare that when one commissioner did show up at the plant, workers there failed to recognize him and ordered him off the premises. For the most part, Smith says, "We did our thing, and they just left us alone."

At this point, the first stage of the Nut Island effect is in place. We have a distracted management and a dedicated team that toils, by choice, in obscurity. They are isolated not only from management but from their customers—in this case, the public. Team members, who share a similar background, value system, and outlook, have enormous trust in each other and very little in outsiders, especially management. Now, an egregious display of indifference from management is all it takes to set the downward spiral in motion.

On Nut Island, this display came in January 1976, when the plant's four gigantic diesel engines shut down. The disaster was predictable. Since the early 1970s, the workers at Nut Island had been warning the top brass in Boston that the engines, which pumped wastewater into the plant and then through a series of aeration and treatment tanks, desperately needed maintenance. The MDC, though, had refused to release any funds to maintain them. Make do with what you have, plant operators were told. When something stops working, we'll find you the money to fix it. In essence, the MDC's management refused to act until a crisis forced their hand. That crisis arrived when the engines gave out entirely. The team at the plant worked frantically to get the engines running again, but for four days, untreated sewage flowed into the harbor.

The incident propelled the conflict between the Nut Island team and senior management from the second stage to the third—from passive resentment to active avoidance. The plant workers viewed the breakdown as a mortifying failure that they could have averted if MDC headquarters had listened to them instead of cutting them adrift. In ordinary circumstances, management's indifference might have killed off the team's morale and motivation. It had the opposite effect on the Nut Islanders. They united around a common adversary. Nut Island was *their* plant, and its continued operation was

solely the result of their own heroic efforts. No bureau-
crat in Boston was going to stop them from running it
the way it ought to be run. (To this day, the workers at
Nut Island deny that their cohesiveness stemmed from
their shared disdain for headquarters; "I don't want to
give them credit for *anything*," one worker told me
recently.)

It became a priority among the Nut Islanders to avoid
contact with upper management whenever possible.
When the plant ran short of ferrous chloride, a chemical
used for odor control, no one from Nut Island asked
headquarters for funds to buy a new supply. Instead, they
would contact a local community activist and ask her to
complain to her state representative about odors ema-
nating from the plant. The rep would then contact MDC
headquarters, and Nut Island would receive a fresh supply of ferrous chloride. In part, this was a case of shrewd
"managing upward" by Bill Smith and his colleagues. But
it also shows how far the team would go to avoid dealing
with management.

Another way the Nut Islanders stayed off management's radar screen was to keep their machinery running
long past the time it should have been overhauled or
junked. Their repairs often showed great ingenuity—at
times they even manufactured their own parts on-site.
Ultimately, though, the team's resourcefulness compro-
mised the very job they were supposed to accomplish.

Among the plant's most troublesome equipment were
the pumps that drew sludge—fecal matter and other
solids—into the digester tanks. Inside the tanks, anaero-
bic bacteria were added to eliminate the pathogens in
the sludge, reduce its volume, and render it safe for
release into the harbor. Years of deferred maintenance

had degraded the pumps, but instead of asking Boston for funds to replace them, the Nut Islanders lubricated the machinery with lavish amounts of oil. Much of this oil found its way into the digester tanks themselves. From there, it was released into the harbor. (Beginning in 1991, treated sludge was shipped to a nearby facility for conversion to fertilizer.) A former sewer division scientist tells me he suspects the releases of tainted sludge account for the high concentration of oil in Boston Harbor's sediments, compared with other harbors on the East Coast.

Rules of Thumb

A team can easily lose sight of the big picture when it is narrowly focused on a demanding task. The task itself becomes the big picture, crowding other considerations out of the frame. To counteract this tendency, smart managers supply reality checks by exposing their people to the perspectives and practices of other organizations. (For other suggestions, see "How to Stop the Nut Island Effect Before It Starts" at the end of this article.) A team in the fourth stage of the Nut Island effect, however, is denied this exposure. Isolated in its lonely outpost, its stock of ideas limited to those of its own members, the team begins to make up its own rules. These rules are terribly insidious because they foster in the team and its management the mistaken belief that its operations are running smoothly.

On Nut Island, one such rule governed the amount of grit—the sand, dirt, and assorted particulate crud that inevitably finds its way into wastewater—that the plant workers considered acceptable. Because of a flaw in the plant's design, its aeration tanks would become choked with grit if the inflow of sewage exceeded a certain volume. The plant operators dealt with this problem by limiting inflows to what they considered a manageable level, diverting the excess into the harbor. Reflecting the distorted perspective typical of teams in the grip of the Nut Island effect, these diversions were not even recorded as overflows from the plant because the excess wastewater did not, strictly speaking, enter the facility.

Another rule of thumb governed the use of chlorine at Nut Island. When inflows were particularly heavy, even the sewage that flowed through the plant did not always undergo full treatment. The plant's operators would add massive amounts of chlorine to some of the wastewater and pipe it out to sea. The chlorine eliminated some pathogens in the wastewater, but its other effects were less benign. Classified by the Environmental Protection Agency as an environmental contaminant, chlorine kills marine life, depletes marine oxygen supplies, and harms fragile shore ecosystems. To the team on Nut Island, though, chlorine was better than nothing. By their reckoning, they were giving the wastewater at least minimal treatment—thus their indignant denials when Quincy residents complained of raw sewage in the water and on their beaches.

In its fifth stage, the Nut Island effect generates its own reality-distortion field. This process is fairly straightforward in management's case. Disinclined in the first place to look too closely at the team's operations, management is easily misled by the team's skillful disguising of its flaws and deficiencies. In fact, it wants to be misled—it has enough problems on its plate. One reason MDC management left Nut Island alone is that even as it was falling apart, the plant looked clean, especially compared to the old Deer Island plant, which suffered a very public series of breakdowns in the 1970s and 1980s. Reassured by Nut Island's patina of efficiency, the MDC's upper management focused on business that seemed more pressing.

The manner in which team members delude themselves is somewhat more complicated. Part of their self-deception involves wishful thinking—the common human tendency to reject information that clashes with the reality one wishes to see. Consider, for instance, the laboratory tests performed at the plant. These tests were required by the EPA, which issues to every sewage plant in the country a permit that spells out how much coliform bacteria and other pollutants can remain in wastewater after it has been treated. A former scientist with the Massachusetts Water Resources Authority tells me the staff in the Nut Island lab would simply ignore unfavorable test results. Their intent was not to deceive the EPA, the scientist hastens to add. "It was more like they looked at the numbers and said, 'This can't be right. Let's test it again.'" This sort of unconscious bias is common in laboratory work, and there are ways to correct for it. On Nut Island, though, the bias went uncorrected. As long as Nut Island's numbers appeared to fall within EPA limits, MDC management in Boston saw no reason to question the plant's testing regimen. To the Nut Islanders themselves, "making the permit" was proof in itself that they were alleviating the harbor's pollution.

Maintaining the alternate reality that prevailed on Nut Island required more than wishful thinking, however. It also involved strenuous denials when outsiders pointed out inconvenient facts. Consider what I learned from David Standley, who for several years was an environmental consultant to the city of Quincy. Tall and spare, with the methodical manner of a born engineer, Standley told me about the state of the plant's digester tanks in 1996.

Under the best of circumstances, sludge is nasty stuff—it scares even sewer workers—and it must be carefully tended and monitored to make sure the treatment process is on track. But everything Standley saw at the plant led him to conclude that the sludge was being handled in the most haphazard, ad hoc manner imaginable, with little concern for producing usable material. Indeed, in 1995 and 1996, the company contracted to convert Boston's sludge to fertilizer rejected 40% of the shipments from Nut Island. Clearly, there was a problem with the digesters. "I remember taking one look at the tanks' operating parameters and saying, 'This is going to die soon,'" Standley says. "When you've got volatile acids in the tanks rising and falling by 20% or more on a daily basis, with no apparent pattern, by definition something is very wrong."

Predictably enough, these misgivings found an unfriendly reception on Nut Island. "Their initial reaction," Standley says, "was hostility—they didn't like me sticking my nose into their business." Besides, they insisted, there was nothing seriously wrong with the digesters. The wide fluctuations in acidity were just one of their little idiosyncrasies. Instead of addressing the root causes of the variances, the team would improvise a quick fix, such as adding large amounts of alkali to the tanks when sample readings (which may or may not have been reliable) indicated high acidity levels.

If external events had not intervened, conditions on Nut Island would probably have continued to deteriorate until the digesters failed or some other crisis erupted. The plant's shutdown in 1997 forestalled that possibility. As part of a large-scale plan to overhaul Greater Boston's sewer system and clean up the harbor, all sewage treatment was shifted to a new, state-of-the-art facility on Deer Island. The Nut Island team was disbanded, after 30 years of effort that left the harbor no cleaner than it was in the late 1960s when the core team first came together.

The field of organizational studies is a well-established discipline with an extensive literature. Yet as far as I can determine, the syndrome that I call the Nut Island effect has, until now, gone unnamed—though not unrecognized, as I learned when I described it to other managers. Perhaps the lack of a name indicates just what a subtle and insidious thing it is; the Nut Island effect itself has flown under the radar of managers and academics just as the actions of team members go unnoticed by management. A common and longstanding feature of many public agencies and private companies, the Nut Island effect is often seen not as a pathology but as part of the normal state of affairs. I am convinced, though, that when good people are put in a situation in which they inexorably do the wrong things, it is not normal or unavoidable. It is tragic. It is a cruel waste of human passion and energy, and a deep-seated threat to an organization's mission and bottom line. That is why it is incumbent upon management to recognize the circumstances that can produce the Nut Island effect and prevent it from taking hold.

Five Steps to Failure

THE NUT ISLAND EFFECT IS A destructive organizational dynamic that pits a homogeneous, deeply committed team against its disengaged senior managers. Their conflict can be mapped as a negative feedback spiral that passes through five predictable stages.

1. Management, its attention riveted on high-visibility problems, assigns a vital, behind-the-scenes task to a team and gives that team a great deal of autonomy. Team members self-select for a strong work ethic and an aversion to the spotlight. They become adept at organizing and managing themselves, and the unit develops a proud and distinct identity.

2. Senior management takes the team's self-sufficiency for granted and ignores team members when they ask for help or try to warn of impending trouble. When trouble strikes, the team feels betrayed by management and reacts with resentment.

3. An us-against-the-world mentality takes hold in the team, as isolation heightens its sense of itself as a band of heroic outcasts. Driven by the desire to stay off management's radar screen, the team grows skillful at disguising its problems. Team members never acknowledge problems to outsiders or ask them for help. Management is all too willing to take the team's silence as a sign that all is well.

4. Management fails in its responsibility to expose the team to external perspectives and practices. As a result, the team begins to make up its own rules. The team tells itself that the rules enable it to fulfill its mission. In fact, these rules mask grave deficiencies in the team's performance.

5. Both management and the team form distorted pictures of reality that are very difficult to correct. Team members refuse to listen when well-meaning outsiders offer help or attempt to point out problems and deficiencies. Management, for its part, tells itself that no news is good news and continues to ignore team members and their task. Management and the team continue to shun each other until some external event breaks the stalemate.

How to Stop the Nut Island Effect Before It Starts

WHAT FORMS OF PREVENTIVE MEDICINE can we prescribe to help organizations avoid the Nut Island effect? Managers need to walk a fine line. The humane values and sense of commitment that distinguished the Nut Island team are precisely the virtues we want to encourage. The trick is to decouple them from the isolation and lack of external focus that breeds self-delusion, counterproductive practices, and, ultimately, failure.

On Nut Island, the workers' focus paralleled their reward system. That system evolved by default as a result of MDC headquarters' lack of interest and by explicit action from dedicated local managers. It rewarded task-driven results—avoid grit in the sedimentation tanks, keep the sludge pumps from seizing up, keep the digesters alive—rather than mission-oriented results—maximize flows to be treated through the plant, produce fertilizer-quality sludge. The Nut Island crew were heroes, but unfortunately they were fighting the wrong war. As in combat, the generals were to blame, not the enlisted personnel.

The striking persistence of the syndrome—which lingered on Nut Island until the plant was shut down in 1997, despite a decade of structural and management changes that afforded the team greater financial resources, new career options, top management support, and other opportunities—should send a strong message to corporate managers. While there are probably ways to counteract the Nut Island effect in your company, you are far better off to avoid it in the first place.

1. The first step is to install performance measures and reward structures tied to both internal operations and companywide goals. The internal links are necessary to help build the team's sense of local responsibility and camaraderie; the link to external goals ensures the proper calibration of internal operations to the corporate mission.

2. Second, senior management must establish a hands-on presence by visiting the team, holding recognition ceremonies, and leading tours of customers or employees from other parts of the organization through the site. These occasions give senior management a chance to detect early warnings of problems and they give the local team a sense that they matter and are listened to.

3. Third, team personnel must be integrated with people from other parts of the organization. This exposes the local team members to ideas and practices being used by colleagues elsewhere in the company or in other organizations. It encourages them to think in terms of the big picture.

4. Finally, outside people—managers and line workers alike—need to be rotated into the team environment. This should occur every two to three years—not so often as to be disruptive but often enough to discourage the institutionalization of bad habits. So as not to appear punitive, this rotation must be a regular feature of corporate life, not a tactic aimed at a particular group.

Originally published in March 2001
Reprint R0103C

About the Contributors

RICHARD BOHMER is a physician and an Assistant Professor at Harvard Business School in Boston.

VANESSA URCH DRUSKAT is an Associate Professor of Organizational Behavior at the Whittemore School of Business and Economics at the University of New Hampshire in Durham.

AMY EDMONDSON is an Associate Professor at Harvard Business School. She teaches M.B.A.'s about managing change and learning in organizations and Ph.D. students about research methods. Professor Edmondson investigates learning in cross-functional teams and has done pioneering research on how psychological safety enables team and organizational learning and process innovation.

DAVID A. GARVIN is the C. Roland Christensen Professor of Business Administration at Harvard Business School in Boston.

JON R. KATZENBACH and DOUGLAS K. SMITH were partners at McKinsey & Company at the time this article was written. They are coauthors of *The Wisdom of Teams*. In addition, Katzenbach has since written six books, the most recent being *Why Pride Matters More Than Money*. He is currently the Senior and Founding Partner of Katzenbach Partners LLC.

PAUL F. LEVY is President and CEO of Beth Israel Deaconess Medical Center in Boston. From 1987 until 1992, he was the Executive Director of the Massachusetts Water Resources Authority.

CHRISTOPHER MEYER founded Nerve to carry on the work of the Center for Business Innovation, which he directed from 1995 until it was closed in 2002. His most recent book is *It's Alive: The Coming Convergence of Information, Biology, and Business.*

GARY PISANO is the Harry E. Figgie, Jr., Professor of Business Administration at Harvard Business School in Boston.

MICHAEL A. ROBERTO is an Assistant Professor at Harvard Business School in Boston.

ISABELLE ROYER is a Professor of Management at the IAE Business School of the University of Lille 1, France, and is affiliated with the university's GREMCO research center, which focuses on organization and strategy issues.

DOUGLAS K. SMITH is recognized in *The Guru Guide* as one of the world's top management consultants. He is the author of *Make Success Measurable, Taking Charge of Change,* and *On Value and Values.*

WILLIAM M. SNYDER is a cofounder of CPsquare, a cross-organizational, cross-sector community of practice on communities of practice. His research and consulting work focuses on community-based learning systems in the civic domain—in areas such as education, public safety, and economic development—both within and across cities at national and international levels.

ETIENNE C. WENGER is a consultant on knowledge management and communities of practice and the author of *Culti-*

vating Communities of Practice: A Guide to Managing Knowledge, coauthored with William Snyder and Richard McDermott. He is based in North San Juan, CA.

STEVEN B. WOLFF is an Assistant Professor of Management and a Partner at Innovative Systems Associates. He can be reached at steve@profwolff.com.

Index

accountability, mutual vs. individual, 2, 5, 13–15
activity teams, 2, 16–18
advocacy process, 101–104
    closure and, 112–114
    vs. inquiry process, 105, 118–121
affective conflict, 104–106, 117
Alberting, Dick, 2
ambiguity, 114
American Express, 117
American Management Systems (AMS), 135–137, 138
AMP Corporation, 40, 43
AMS. *See* American Management Systems (AMS)
assumptions, 109, 115–116
Aussedat Rey, 60–62
awareness of emotions, 30
    in groups, 36–38
    in individuals, 32–34, 45
    in organizations, 40–44

bad projects, persistence of, 53–76. *See also* collective belief; Nut Island effect

cases of, 56–63
    project appeal and, 63–68
    steps for avoiding, 68–73
balanced scorecard, 152–153
Batten, Jim, 3
Bay of Pigs invasion, 118–120
best practices, transfer of, 140–141
Buckman Labs, 140
Burlington Northern Railroad, 2, 12
business development, and communities of practice, 139–140
Business Roundtable, 127

"call the question," 114
cardiac surgery, new technology in, 91–95. *See also* surgical teams
caring behavior, 35
Castro, Fidel, 119
Chrysler, 111, 140–141
CIA, 119
closure, 100, 112–114
coalitions, 107, 109

cognitive conflict, 104–106
cohesiveness. *See also* group
    identity, sense of
    dangers of collective belief
        and, 69
    individuality and, 34–35
    Nut Island effect and,
        177–178
collaboration, 85–86
collective belief, 55, 73–74
    appeal of, 63–68
    avoidance of dangers of,
        68–73
    in bad project cases, 54,
        56–63
    consequences of, 66–68
    emergence of, 64–65
    internal controls and, 69–70
    persistence of, 65–66
    role of exit champion and,
        70–73
collective work product, 4
commitment, shared, 1, 167,
    175
communication, 42, 106–107.
    See also feedback
communities of practice,
    123–142
    characteristics of, 126–132
    defined, 123, 124–125
    examples of, 129–132
    identification of, 133–134
    infrastructure and, 134–137
    managerial paradox in,
        125–126, 132–138
    potential for, 138

types of value added by,
    139–142
completion deadlines, 15, 17
composition of teams
    avoidance of project disas-
        ters and, 54, 56, 69, 186
    communities of practice
        and, 128, 135–136
    process measures and,
        149–150
    team learning and, 85–86
conflict. *See also* Nut Island
    effect
    advocacy perspective and,
        102–103
    cognitive vs. affective,
        104–106
    decision making and, 100,
        104–110
    inquiry perspective and, 103,
        104–110
confrontation, 35, 45
Connell, James W., 176
consideration, 100, 110–112
contracts between teams and
    management, 154–155
control procedures, 67, 69–70
Corning, 57
corporate culture. *See* organi-
    zational culture
"critical delivery points," 17
Cuban Missile Crisis, 118,
    120–121
customers, 45, 58. *See also* out-
    side relationships
Cyrus the Great, 118

DaimlerChrysler, 111, 141
"dashboard" format, 148,
    158–164
debate. *See also* conflict
    merits of, 116–117
    structuring of, 106–107, 108
decision making, 99–121
    advocacy approach and, 99,
        101–104, 118–121
    closure and, 100, 112–114
    consideration and, 100,
        110–112
    as event vs. process, 100–101
    inquiry approach and,
        99–100, 101–104
    process assessment and,
        115–118
    productive conflict and, 100,
        104–110
    team composition and, 11
defensiveness, 32–33
discipline of teams, 1–25
    common approach and,
        12–13
    common purpose and, 5–7
    composition and, 10–11
    mutual accountability and,
        13–15
    performance goals and,
        7–10
    teams defined and, 2–5
diversity, 126–127

EI (emotional intelligence). *See*
    group emotional intelli-
    gence

Eli Lilly, Peripheral Systems
    Division, 8–9
Emerson Electric, 106
Emotional Intelligence (Gole-
    man), 30. *See also* group
    emotional intelligence
Enron, 109–110
enterprise resource planning
    (ERP), 90
enthusiasm, 67, 68–69, 70
ERP. *See* enterprise resource
    planning (ERP)
Essilor, 54, 64, 74
    case study of, 56–60
    collective belief at, 65–67
    exit vs. project champions
        at, 75–76
    safeguards and, 69, 70, 71, 72
exit champion, 54, 56, 70–73,
    75–76
expertise
    communities of practice
        and, 126, 134, 141
    skill development and, 141
    team composition and, 11
    team learning and, 83, 85–86

facts, 109, 115–116
failed projects. *See* bad proj-
    ects, persistence of; Nut
    Island effect
fairness, 110, 114, 117–118. *See*
    also consideration
feedback
    emotional intelligence and,
        37, 38, 45

feedback (*continued*)
   exit champion and, 70–73
   groupthink and, 113
   "intellectual watchdogs"
      and, 115–116, 119
   negative, and collective
      belief, 55, 57, 62, 65–66
   Nut Island effect and, 174,
      179, 186
   performance and, 24–25
   "skeptical generalists" and,
      119
   team learning and, 87–89
first impressions, 22–23
flexibility, 86
focus
   communities of practice
      and, 134
   on team performance, 17–18
Ford Motor Company,
   150–152, 155
framing
   emotional intelligence and,
      42
   productive conflict and, 107
   team learning and, 86–87

Galvin, Bob, 106
General Motors (GM), 113
goals. *See* performance goals
Goldman, Sachs, 20
Goleman, Daniel, 3
Golub, Harvey, 117
Greenwood, Bill, 2
group efficacy, sense of, 29, 31,
   47, 49

group emotional intelligence,
   27–51
   concept of emotional intelli-
      gence and, 28–29
   enhancement of, 50–51
   group emotions and, 36–40
   importance of, 29–30
   individual emotions and,
      32–36, 45
   levels of interaction and,
      30–32
   model for, 44–46
   norms for, 47–50
   organizational relations and,
      40–44
group identity, sense of, 29, 31,
   47, 173–175
groups. *See* working groups
"groupthink," 112–113
Grove, Andy, 110, 113

Hay Group, 27, 34, 39–40, 47
"helpful Cassandras," 113
Hewlett-Packard, 20, 27
   communities of practice
      and, 130–132
   Medical Products Group, 2
   performance ethic at, 13–14
   team emotional intelligence
      and, 33
Hill's Pet Nutrition, 129–130
Holmes, Ben, 2
Hume, David, 116–117
humor, 35, 45–46

IBM, 141

IDEO, 27, 44–46, 50
individual emotions
  awareness of, 32–34, 45
  regulation of, 34–36, 45
informal networks, 128, 133
information
  decision-making closure
    and, 114
  Nut Island effect and,
    181–183
  productive conflict and,
    109–110
  team performance and,
    23–24
infrastructure, and communi-
    ties of practice, 134–137
inquiry process, 101–104
  vs. advocacy process, 105,
    118–121
Intel, 110
"intellectual watchdogs,"
    115–116, 119
internal controls, 84. *See also*
    performance measures
interpersonal skills, 11, 32–33.
    See also group emotional
    intelligence

Kaplan, Robert S., 152–153
Kennedy, John F., 118–121
Kennedy, Robert, 119, 120
Knight, Chuck, 106
Knight-Ridder, 3, 20
"knowledge bank," 136
KoSa (chemical company), 42,
    43

Kucikas, Tony, 174

Lafarge, 54, 74
  case study of, 60–63
  collective belief at, 64–66, 67,
    74
  safeguards and, 69, 70, 71,
    72
language, and conflict, 107
leaders of teams. *See also* exit
    champion
  communities of practice
    and, 133, 135, 138
  conflict management and,
    106–110
  decision-making processes
    and, 101, 106–110, 111,
    112–113, 114, 117–118
  group emotional intelligence
    and, 47, 50
  team learning and, 84,
    89–91, 96–97
leveling. *See also* consideration
  decision-making processes
    and, 119–120
  group emotional intelligence
    and, 50
  team learning and, 87–89
Levi Strauss, 20
Lilly. *See* Eli Lilly, Peripheral
    Systems Division
listening
  level of, 117
  true consideration and,
    110–112
"logic of illogic," 106

MacKinnon, Frank, 173–174
Madden, Jack, 173–174
Malcolm Baldrige National
    Quality Program, 106
management of teams. *See also*
    leaders of teams; senior
    management
    communities of practice
        and, 125–126, 132–138
    team learning and, 83–84,
        86–89
"managing upward," 178
Massachusetts Water
    Resources Authority, 175
MDC. *See* Metropolitan Dis-
    trict Commission (MDC)
Metropolitan District Commis-
    sion (MDC), 175, 177, 185
mission, vs. team purpose,
    19–20
Morton, Dean, 2
motivation, 9
Motorola, 13–14, 106

norms, and team emotional
    intelligence
    attitudes and, 39–40
    caring behavior and, 35–36,
        49
    common vocabulary and, 39
    confrontation and, 35, 45,
        49
    feedback and, 37, 38, 48
    humor and, 35, 39
    importance of, 29
    interpersonal understanding
        and, 32–33, 48

organizational understand-
    ing and, 41–42, 48
perspective taking and,
    33–34, 48
proactive problem solving
    and, 40, 49
self-evaluation and, 37–38,
    48
sources of, 47–50
stress outlets and, 39, 45–46
work environment and,
    39–40, 49
Norton, David P., 152–153
Nut Island effect, 167–186
    defined, 170–171
    management disregard of
        team and, 170–171, 184
    pattern found in, 167–168,
        169–170
    prevention of, 185–186
    reality distortion and, 171,
        180–183, 184
    rules of thumb and, 171,
        179–183, 184
    steps to failure in, 170–171,
        183–184
    story behind, 172–179
    team isolation and, 167–168,
        170–171, 176–177, 184
    us-against-them mentality
        and, 171, 184

Only the Paranoid Survive
    (Grove), 110
organizational culture, 65, 74
    group emotional intelligence
        and, 47, 50

Nut Island effect and,
169–170
organizational relations, 40–44,
49
organizational structure
communities of practice
and, 127–129
team opportunities in, 20–21
"out of bounds" management
review, 154
outside relationships, 40–44,
45, 46, 58
Outward Bound, 9, 38

Pall Corp, 20
Pepsi, 20
performance goals
attainability of, 8–9, 23
decision-making process
and, 116
motivation and, 9, 14–15
performance measures and,
150–152, 156
specificity and, 8, 9
successful teams and, 1,
23
translation from purpose to,
7–10
performance measures,
143–166
auditing and, 157–158, 164
communities of practice
and, 137–138
cross-functional activities
and, 145
"dashboard" for, 148,
158–164

design of, 144, 146, 156–158,
164–166
guiding principles for,
146–148
importance of, 147–149
number of, 144, 147–148
Nut Island effect and, 186
process measures and,
145–147, 149, 164–166
purpose of, 145, 146
results measures and, 145,
149–152
role of senior management
and, 144, 152–155
traditional measures and,
143, 147
perspective taking, 33–34
Platt, Lew, 2
point-counterpoint technique,
115
problem solving, 11, 40, 140
"procedural justice," 110. *See
also* consideration
process measures, 145–147,
149, 164–166. *See also* performance measures
productive conflict, 100,
104–110
professional development, 141
project champion, 56, 64–65,
75–76
projects, mistaken. *See* bad
projects, persistence of
psychological safety, and team
learning, 87–89
purpose
common, 1, 5–7

purpose (*continued*)
  communities of practice
    and, 128
  vs. company mission, 19–20
  performance and, 7–10, 22

quality circles, 15
Quantum Corporation,
    158–164
Quincy, MA. *See* Nut Island
    effect

RCA SelectaVision project,
    54–55, 73–74
recommendation teams, 2,
    15–16
recruitment, 142
regulation of emotions, 30
  in groups, 38–40, 45–46
  in individuals, 34–36, 45
results measures, 145, 149–152
review process
  avoidance of project disas-
    ters and, 54, 56, 69–70
  in bad project cases, 59–60,
    62–63
  "out of bounds" manage-
    ment review and, 154
  performance measures and,
    153–155
  team learning and, 84, 88
reward systems
  communities of practice
    and, 136
  Nut Island effect and, 186
  team performance and,
    24–25

risk
  exit champion and, 76
  team approach and, 18–19
role playing, 109
Rossotti, Charles, 135
rules of conduct, 23
rules of thumb, 171, 179–183

Schrempp, Jurgen, 111
self-censorship, 65–66
self-evaluation, 37–38, 45. *See
    also* performance mea-
    sures
senior management. *See also*
    management of teams;
    teams at the top
  communities of practice
    and, 124, 133, 134–137
  determination of best
    approach and, 2, 18–19
  exit champion, 72–73
  Nut Island effect and,
    167–168, 170–171,
    175–176, 180–181, 186
  performance measures and,
    152–155, 158
  recommendation teams and,
    15–16
  team learning and, 83–84
  team performance and,
    17–18
Shell Oil Company, 133, 138
Sherwin Williams, 37
size of teams, 10–11, 127
"skeptical generalists," 119
skill mix, and team composi-
    tion, 11–12. *See also* com-

position of teams; expertise

Sloan, Alfred, 113

small wins, 9

Smith, Bill, 173–174, 178

"social skills." *See* group emotional intelligence

Sorenson, Theodore, 119

sponsors, and communities of practice, 135, 136

staffing levels, as process measure, 149–150, 160, 163

Standley, David, 181–182

status within teams, 9. *See also* leveling

strategy
communities of practice and, 139
team performance measures and, 144, 150–152, 153

stress, outlets for, 39, 45–46

surgical teams
cardiac surgery technology and, 91–93
factors in learning by, 83–84
impacts of new technology on, 80–81
new technology implementation and, 82–89
parallels between business teams and, 89–91
plug-in technology and, 93–95
speed of learning and, 82–83
team process and, 78–80
technology as innovation project and, 93, 94, 95–96

talent retention, 142

team-building exercises, 38

team learning, 77–97. *See also* professional development; surgical teams; training
communities of practice and, 131–132
factors in, 83–84, 85–89, 90–91
leaders of teams and, 84, 89–91, 96–97
parallels between surgical and business teams and, 89–91
team design and, 85–86
team management and, 86–89

team performance. *See also* performance goals; performance measures
approaches to building, 22–25
focus on, 17–18
vs. work groups, 2

teams
basic categories of, 2, 15–21 (*see also* activity teams; recommendation teams; teams at the top)
communities of practice and, 127–129
emotions of, 36–40, 45–46 (*see also* group emotional intelligence)
as units of performance, 5
working groups and, 4–5, 6, 128

teams at the top, 2, 18–21. *See also* senior management

technology implementation. *See* surgical teams; team learning

"thought leaders," 135

"time-outs," 107

time together, 24

training. *See also* professional development; surgical teams; team learning

design of performance measures and, 144

group emotional intelligence and, 47, 50

trust, mutual, 29, 31, 47

uncertainty, 114

U.S. Army, 107

U.S. Veterans Administration, 134

values, 3–4

Veterans Health Administration Center for Leadership and Development, 37–38, 39

vocabulary, common, 39

voice, 110–111

Wisdom of Teams, The (Katzenbach and Smith), 3. *See also* discipline of teams

Wolfensohn, James, 136

work, common approach to, 12–13, 156

work environment

emotional intelligence and, 39–40, 49

learning and, 87–89

working groups

communities of practice and, 128

compared with teams, 4–5, 6, 128

team option and, 18

World Bank, 135, 136–137, 139